CUM DUDUM

A letter to the Armenians

Benedict XII,
Pope of Rome

Translated by: D.P. Curtin

Dalcassian Publishing Company
PHILADELPHIA, PA

Copyright @ 2021 Dalcassian Publishing Company

All rights reserved. No part of this publication may be reproduced, distributed, or transmitted in any form or by any means, including photocopying, recording, or other electronic or mechanical methods, without the prior written permission of the publisher, except in the case of brief quotations embodied in critical reviews and certain other non-commercial uses permitted by copyright law. For permission request, write to Dalcassian Publishing Company at dalcassianpublishing at gmail.com

ISBN: 979-8-8691-7327-0 (Paperback)

Library of Congress Control Number:
Author: Curtin, D.P. (1985-)

Printed by Ingram Content Group, 1 Ingram Blvd, La Vergne, Tennessee

First printing edition 2021.

CUM DUDUM

CUM DUDUM (Aug. 1, 1341)

A letter to the Armenians

In the name of God. Amen.

When not long ago he came to the audience of the most holy father and our lord, Lord Benedict, by the divine providence of Pope XII, and even long before, while he was appointed to the office of Cardinal, he had very often arrived at the audience of the happy memory of his predecessor, our lord, Pope John XXII, that the Armenians in and about those things which lead to faith and belonging to the Christian faith, commonly in both Armenia or specially in Lesser Armenia, or something about one or the other they held and taught or even preached various and diverse errors, both against the divine Scriptures, the general councils, and also against what it has been taught of the holy Roman Church, the mother and teacher of all, and all the thing she teaches and preaches. Our lord the same pope, wishing to inquire into the aforesaid and their individuals, and to know more fully the truth, caused many Armenians to come to his presence; and the tenants, he caused to come to him, from whom, the Armenians and the Latins, that is to say, from some of them, through the aforesaid lord, the pope, and from others through the reverend father, lord Bernard of the title of Saint Cyriaci, cardinal priest in Thermae, on the command of the lord the pope himself, there existed an oath, which upon the aforesaid and upon others what they had heard or known to hold, teach or preach in the said parts or elsewhere from the same Armenians, full and simple, both about themselves, as about the principals, and about other persons, living and deceased, so that the witnesses would confess and depose the truth. Having thus received them, and after them, those who could neither speak nor understand the Latin language, through suitable interpreters and others who knew how to speak and understand both languages. Namely, Armenian and Latin, by themselves as well as by certain books written in the Armenian language. They themselves handed down to our pope by some of the said Armenians, to whom, as many of the same Armenians asserted and still assert, the Armenians commonly use both in Greater Armenia and in the Lesser. They carefully examined, for these things assigned to them a certain apostolic notary, who took depositions and confessions while they were made and errors certain while they were interpreting or extracting from the aforesaid books, by certain persons both languages, both Armenian and Latin, knowing how to understand and speak, he redacted and redacted in writings. Consequently, from their depositions and confessions, it was found that the Armenians, or some of them, hold, believe, and teach the articles below:

I. And first, that some of the ancient teachers of the Armenians said and preached, that the Holy Spirit proceeds from the Son as well as from the Father; may proceed from the Son as well as from the Father, because at the said time a council was held among the Armenians, where there were Catholicons and bishops and teachers of the Armenians and the patriarch of the Syrians, and there they determined that it should not be said among them that the Holy Spirit should proceed from the Son as from the Father ; and they condemned the ancient teachers of the Armenians, who were before the aforesaid council, because they had said and taught that the Holy Spirit proceeds from the Son as well as from the Father. and from that time all the Armenians who held and taught that the Holy Spirit proceeded from the Son, as well as from the Father, were persecuted, imprisoning them and putting them in chains. And so, among the Armenians no one dares to say or teach this, except only those <who> are united to the holy Roman Church. And if it is sometimes found in their books that the Holy Spirit proceeds from the Son, they say that this procession of time, to sanctify the creature, and not of his eternal procession, by which he proceeded eternally from the Father and the Son into being personally, is to be understood.

II. Also, that the Armenians, the article of faith placed in the Symbol concerning the Holy Spirit, pronounce thus: I believe in the Holy Spirit, uncreated and perfect, who spoke in the Law and the Prophets and the Gospels and descended in the Jordan and preached in the Apostles and dwells in the Saints - making no mention, that the Holy Spirit proceeds from the Father or from the Father and the Son. - However, when they read the Gospel of John, where it is said that the Paraclete proceeds from the Father, they say and confess this; but many of them deny that the Holy Spirit proceeds from the Son; and if some believe this, yet they dare not say it plainly. And although it was not expressly determined in the Council of Chalcedon that the Holy Spirit proceeded from the Son as from the Father, but this had been determined in the Councils of Constantinople and Ephesus because the Council of Chalcedon nevertheless approved the determinations made in the said previous councils, therefore, rejecting the said Council of Chalcedon, the said Armenians rejected the said councils which were approved by the said council, among which was that the Holy Spirit proceeds from the Son as well as from the Father.

III. Also, that in the said council they rejected the Council of Chalcedon principally from what had been determined in the said Council of Chalcedon, that in the Lord Jesus Christ there were two natures, namely, human and divine, and a single person subsisting in two natures; and in the said council they determined that just as there was one person in the Lord Jesus Christ, so there was one nature, that is, divine, and one will and one operation, and they anathematized saying the contrary. and those who said the contrary were persecuted, imprisoning them, binding them, and putting them to death. In the said council they also condemned *the blessed* Pope Leo and his letters which he had sent to the Council of Chalcedon and to the Patriarch Flavian of Constantinople, in which the blessed Leo had written that in the Lord Jesus Christ there were two natures and one person, two wills and two operations. In the said council of the Dioscians, they canonized him who had been condemned by the said council of Chalcedon, and wanted to be considered a saint, and they still celebrate him three times a year as a saint and praise him as a saint. and they curse the blessed Leo and the council of Chalcedon, who condemned the saying of Dioscorus. They also say that those who agreed to the determinations of the said Council of Chalcedon denied Christ.

IV. Also, what the Armenians say and hold, that the personal sin of their first parents was so grievous, that all their children propagated from their seed, until the suffering of Christ, were rightfully condemned for their personal sin, and were cast into hell after death, not because of the fact that they themselves contracted some original sin from Adam, when they say that children have no original sin at all, neither before nor after Christ's passion; but the said damnation followed them before Christ's passion because of the gravity of their personal sin, which Adam and Eve committed by transgressing the divine commandment given to them, but after the Lord's passion, in which the sin of the first parents was erased, the children who are born from the sons of Adam are not bound to damnation, nor to hell On account of the said sin, they are to be pushed away, because Christ completely wiped out the sin of the first parents in his passion.

V. Also, that a certain teacher of the Armenians called Mechitariz, which is translated Paraclete, introduced anew and taught that the human soul of a son is propagated from the soul of his father, as a body from a body, and an angel also from another; because, since the existing rational human soul and the existing angel of the intellectual nature are certain spiritual lights, they propagate other spiritual lights from themselves; and in this they follow him, as it were, from the province of Argicienus, which is a large province, containing seven provinces. But other Armenians do not say this, but that God creates all souls. And the Armenians of the said province have that Mechitariz as a Saint.

VI. Likewise, the Armenians say that the souls of children who are born of Christian parents after Christ's passion, if they die before being baptized, go to the earthly paradise in which Adam was before sin. but the souls of children who are born of non-Christian parents after Christ's passion and die without baptism, go to the places where the souls of their parents are.

VII. Also, what the said Armenians say, that the souls of adult men, who have died or will die after the passion of Christ, go to the air or to the earth, which is next to the earthly paradise, or elsewhere, where God orders them to remain until the day of judgment, whether they are Christians. or not; yet none of their souls goes to hell, or to the heavenly or earthly paradise, until the aforesaid time of Judgment. And, as they say, the souls of unbaptized children will come to the General Judgment with their bodies, and after the judgment they will go to the earthly paradise, in which they will fly like doves from one tree to another and like angels from heaven to earth and from one part of the earth to another. Yet they will not have glory, nor will they endure any punishment. After the general judgment, the souls of the adults will go to the places that will be assigned to them after the general Judgment.

VIII. Also, what the Armenians say, that the souls of baptized children and the souls of many perfect men after the General Judgment will enter the kingdom of heaven, where they will be free from all the punishing evils of this life, because they will neither hunger nor thirst nor feel the other defects of the human body, neither marry nor be married, they will sit as the angels of God in the heavens will not be able to sin or fall from the state in which they were. However, they will not see the essence of God, because no creature can see it; but they will see the brightness of God, which flows from his essence, just as the light of the sun emanates from the sun, and yet it is not the sun; and in the said vision there will be different degrees of the said brightness, so that the angels will see the said brightness more perfectly than any man, and prophets and apostles and martyrs and virgins, than baptized children; and in this they say that the happiness of perfect saints and of baptized children consists.

IX. Likewise, of unbaptized children and of men not perfectly righteous, who, of course, have not reached the perfection of apostles, martyrs, confessors, and virgins, the Armenians say that after the General Judgment they will go to an earthly and not a heavenly paradise, where they will be free from all bodily discomfort and will delight among the trees of paradise; yet they will neither eat nor drink nor marry nor be given in marriage, and so they will remain there forever, and their happiness consists in this. However, there will be a difference between unbaptized Christian children, children and adults who are not perfectly righteous; because adults who are not perfectly righteous will have a crown from the light of the fire with which the earth will be burned before the Judgment; they will also see the brightness of the wood of the Cross of Christ, which brightness will then be greatest; because all the luminaries that are in this world will be joined to the luminosity of the Cross of Christ, and the said adults, according as they will be more or less perfect, will have the said crowns of light and will see the said luminosity of the Cross of Christ differently, according to their merits; yet unbaptized children will not have the said crowns of light, nor will they see the brightness of the Cross of Christ; and in this there will be a difference between them.

X. They also say that, on average, bad Christians will not go to the heavenly or earthly paradise after the General Judgment, but will remain in the land where men now live, which will be full of trees, like an earthly paradise, and yet they will neither eat nor drink nor from then on they will die; and this place will be given to them from the fact that they were moderately bad. But they call men moderately bad, married men and others living in common in the world.

XI. Likewise, concerning many bad men, as are generally all unbelievers and Christians, who lead a bad and sinful life, they have two opinions, one of which is, that such after the General Judgment will be put into the Ocean, which will then be fiery, and there they will be severely tortured by the worms that will be there, who will be as great as dragons; and as they have sinned more or less, the so-called dragons will be either greater or lesser; because, as they say, immediately when a man sins grievously, the so-called dragon is born in the ocean and grows according to how much the man sins more or less; and some of the wicked men, who have committed many sins and divers things, will have several dragons there, one of which will torment them in the eyes and the other in the ears, and so on in other parts. The demons who will be there with them will also be crucified there, according to what the Lord is going to say to the wicked: *Go into the eternal fire, which is prepared for the devil and his angels;* and thus, evil men will be tormented there forever. But another opinion of theirs says, which is more common among the Armenians, that after the general judgment there will be no hell, nor is it mine, nor was it after Christ descended to the underworld and completely destroyed hell, but every sinner will be tormented for the sin he has committed, and according to that he has sinned more or less, according to this he will be tormented more or less by said sins; and thus such sins are said to be Hell, in which sinners will be tormented after the General Judgment.

XII. Also, the aforesaid Armenians say that men who are moderately bad are placed in the judgment with their works in the balance, and if they weigh more of their evils than their good, then they are put into the ocean, according to the aforesaid opinion of which it was said above, and they suffer there according to what they have deserved. But if they weigh their good more than their bad, then they will be placed in that land, which will be full of trees, but not so pleasant as the earthly paradise. But if they weigh their good and their evil equally, then through the prayers of the Blessed Mary and other Saints, God will place them in that land where no afflictive evil will be tolerated.

XIII Also, although it is contained in the Ordinarial of the Armenians, that those who are baptized, even if they are children, who come to baptism from the devil's servitude, yet they say that such children have no sin, but as if completely innocent and immune from all sin, even original; nor do they say that they are baptized, that they may obtain the remission of sins, but that they may be Christians, and that after the General Judgment they may enter with the perfect Saints into the kingdom of heaven; and for these two things baptism is valid for them according to them.

XIV. Likewise, what the said Armenians say and hold, that Christ descending to hell preached there and justified those souls who wanted to believe him but left those who did not want to believe him in their sin. Coming out of hell, he completely destroyed hell and all the souls he found there, whether they were good or bad, he brought out from there and placed them in this air and earth and around the earthly paradise, where they will be until the final judgment. In the meantime, however, souls moderately bad and simply bad do not suffer any sensible punishment, but only fear; moderately evil indeed, because they fear their danger, which will be in the day of judgment, as is written above, when they are placed in the balance; but the evil simply because they fear the punishment of the Ocean, where they will be placed after the General Judgment, suffer the punishment of fear, which afflicts them much mentally. But he placed moderately good and perfectly good things in that earth or in the air around the earthly paradise; and, as they say, such souls are in great consolation because of the hope they have of the reward they will obtain after the general Judgment. And they say that before the said General Judgment there will be no other reward for good or bad works, leading to this saying of the Apostle: It *is necessary for us to be presented before the judgment seat of Christ, so that each one may receive according to what he has done in the body, whether it was good or bad.*

XV. Also, what the said Armenians do not say or maintain, that Christ descending to hell preached to the demons, nor that he brought the demons out of Hell, but they say well that the demons are in that air or on earth until the General Judgment. If, however, those present there endure or will endure any sensible punishment until the said General Judgment, they do not express it; they say, however, that they suffer a lack of glory, and that they, who were formerly famous, have been made black; and that they greatly fear the punishment of the Ocean, in which they will be placed after the General Judgment with evil men.

XVI. Also, that among the Armenians there are two opinions about the time when the angels were created; because some of them say that angels were created before this sensible world; but others say that they were created with this sensible world, that is, with the imperial heaven, before every day. They also say that all the angels were created good and stood in the said goodness, as some of them say, until the fourth day, when God made the lights; but some of them say that on the sixth day, when Adam was created, the demons sinned and fell from heaven through that part of heaven which is called among them Arocea, but with us it is called Galaxy; with whom one good angel also fell through the aforesaid hole, and many others would have fallen, had not God said to them: *Peace be unto you,* but that good angel who had fallen, at the prayers of the blessed Basil, was restored to heaven. Some of them also say that Adam was created from nothing on Friday, but about the sixth of the said day Eve was formed, and according to some of them she was tempted by the devil on the same day, and according to others on Friday of the following week. They also say that none of the good angels will ever become evil, and no evil good.

XVII. Also, what the Armenians commonly hold is that there is no purgatory for souls in another world, because, as they say, if a Christian confesses his sins, all his sins and the punishments of his sins are forgiven him. Nor do they themselves pray for the dead, that their sins may be forgiven in another world, but they pray generally for all the dead, as for blessed Mary, the apostles, martyrs and other saints, that on the day of judgment they may enter the heavenly kingdom or in other places, as was said above, and that they may rest there. But of the souls of the pagans, they say that their souls are on their graves or in their graves until the day of judgment, and voices and groans are frequently heard in the graves of the Saracens, and even sometimes their souls or demons are seen for them around their graves in different species of animals or men. for which reason the Saracens do not willingly stand near the graves of the Saracens, and for this reason also sometimes the Saracens cause their children to be baptized and anointed in different places, so that they do not come out of the graves after death. yet they do not cause them to be baptized, that they may become Christians.

XVIII. Likewise, what the Armenians believe and hold is that Christ came down from heaven and was incarnated for the salvation of men, not because the children propagated from Adam and Eve after their sin contract from them the original sin, from which they are saved through the incarnation and death of Christ, when they say that there is no such sin in the sons of Adam, but they say that Christ was incarnated and suffered for the salvation of men, because by his passion the sons of Adam, who preceded the said passion, were freed from Hell in which they were, not by reason of original sin, which was in them. but on account of the gravity of the personal sin of the first parents. They also believe that Christ was incarnated and suffered for the sake of the salvation of the children who were born after his passion, because through his passion he completely destroyed hell, and thus after his passion none of the said children goes to hell. They also believe that Christ was incarnated and suffered for the salvation of adult Christian men, because if such people repent of their sins after his suffering, when they die, they do not go to hell.

XIX. Also, what the Armenians believe and hold, that the first parents and all their posterity until Christ's passion was dead in body and soul descended to Hell, not because of the original sin that the children of Adam contracted from Adam, but because of the gravity of the personal sin of the first parents. for which reason, although their children had not sinned, yet because of the sin of their first parents they had suffered bodily death, and their souls were punished in the underworld until the said time. They also believe and hold that after Christ's passion and before, until the general resurrection, the sons of Adam have an inordinate lust of the flesh and mortality because of the gravity of the sin of their first parents and not because of the original sin they contracted from them. from which concupiscence and mortality, the Saints will be freed in the general resurrection through Christ; and to this extent they say that the so-called lust of the flesh is a sin and an evil, that even Christian parents commit a sin when they have matrimonial intercourse. And for this reason, penance is imposed on them by the priests, because they say that the matrimonial act is a sin and also marriage. They also believe and hold that if Adam and Eve had not transgressed God's command, there would not have been carnal intermingling between them, nor would the human generation have occurred through the intermingling of seeds, but men would have propagated from men without carnal mixing, as light is propagated from light. They also say that God, foreseeing that men would transgress his commandment, made genital organs in them, by means of which the propagation of men would take place after sin.

XX. Again, what the Armenians believe and hold, that the eternal Son of God, born of the substance of the Father, in time united to himself the human nature and became man, even so, because in the very union of the human nature to the Son of God, the human nature was converted into his divine nature. so that after the said union there is in Christ only one nature, that is to say, divine and not human, just as he is one person. And the said Armenians curse all those who say the contrary, and to the extent they detest those who say that after the union there are two natures in Christ, viz., the divine and the human; that if any Armenian, previously baptized according to their rite, should say this, they do not commune with him, but regard him as if he had been a heathen; and if he wishes to return to the faith of the Armenians, they rebaptize him, so that he would always have been a heathen, and after the second baptism they impose on him a penance of twenty years.

XXI Also, what the Armenians believe and hold, that because according to them, after the union of the natures in Christ, human nature was converted into the divine nature, so that from that time there was nothing but the divine nature in Christ, since the said divine nature in Christ was passible and impassible. mortal and immortal, according as it pleased Christ, so they say that Christ suffered and died according to the divine nature, because he so willed, although the human nature was not in him when he suffered and died. They also believe and hold that in the Lord Jesus Christ after the union there was only one understanding, one will and one operation, that is to say, divine and not human.

XXII. Also, what the Armenians say and hold, that from that hour when the Lord died on the cross, he himself descended to the underworld and completely destroyed Hell. so that from that time there was no Hell, nor were any souls of men or even demons in Hell from that time, nor will they be afterwards; But when Christ rose again, bringing out of hell the souls of the saints who were there, he led them into the earthly paradise and entered with them the said paradise, saying to them: *Behold the place where you were;* and immediately he drove them out of the said paradise and placed them on the earth or in the air around the earthly paradise.

XXIII. Likewise, as to the soul of the thief who confessed Christ on the cross, among the Armenians there are different opinions: one of which is that what is said in the Gospel: *Today you will be with me in paradise; today,* it is not held there determinedly for that day when the Lord and the thief were dead, but it is held for the day of the final judgment, when the perfect saints will enter the heavenly paradise, as the day is taken in the psalm: A day *is better than one in your courts* ; for then, and not before, the thief will enter the heavenly paradise, according to them, with other perfect saints. But another opinion of theirs says that on the day on which the said thief died, his soul came to the gate of the earthly paradise, desiring to enter there; but by angels and Enoch and Elijah he was forbidden to enter there; but on the day of the Lord's resurrection, when the Lord came with the other souls of the Saints, whom he had taken out of Hell, to the gate of the earthly paradise, he found there the so-called soul of a thief, and when the Lord had shown his hands and sides to the angels and Enoch and Elijah, opening the gate of paradise to him, he entered there when the said soul of the robber and of the other Saints had said with them: *Behold the place from which you came forth;* He went out of paradise with all the said souls and placed them on the earth or in the air around the said paradise, where they will be until the day of judgment. and then they will be introduced into the heavenly paradise. Others, however, say that at that hour when Adam left paradise on Friday, the Lord placed the soul of the thief in the earthly paradise; whether, however, afterwards he brought her out thence or not, they do not say.

XXIV. Also, what the said Armenians say and hold, that the souls of bad men, who committed many serious actual sins, who died before the Passion of Christ, were placed in Hell, and there endured the infernal punishments for their sins; but when the Lord destroyed Hell after his Passion, he placed the said souls on earth or in the air; and there they go hither and thither, not enduring any sensible punishment, until the day of judgment. But the souls of the evil men who were after the Passion of the Lord, when the said men are dead, evil and terrible angels take them and bring them to the Ocean, of which mention was made above, and show them the Ocean and the worms or dragons that are there; and they say to them that after the General Judgment they will be placed there and through the said Ocean and the dragons will be tortured; and from this the said souls fear much because of the said punishments which they will suffer after the General Judgment; but in the meantime they will not endure another sensible punishment. But the souls of good and perfect men, when they have died, are received by good angels and taken to heaven before the throne of God; and they see under the throne of God, which is the throne of angels, the glory which they will have after the general judgment; and they take great comfort in this; afterwards, however, they are taken by the angels to the earth or to the air, and are there until the day of judgment, and are said to rest because of the said hope. They also say and believe that after the General Judgment, evil men, who were either before or after the Lord's Passion, will be placed in body and soul in the said Ocean, and there they will be tormented forever.

XXV. Also, because the Armenians say that there is only one nature in Christ, that is, divine and not human, they cannot answer to the sayings placed in the Scriptures, by which it is clearly shown that Christ had a human soul, which was not a divine nature, as: *I will not leave my soul in hell* ; nor to that: *My beloved is sad unto death* ; nor to that which Peter says, that he descended spiritually, and preached in Hell; nor to that which the Lord says: *Father, into thy hands I commend my spirit, and bowing his head he gave up his spirit.* By all which the Scripture plainly says, the human soul was in Christ after the union. But when the aforesaid is said to them, not having anything to answer, they have recourse to sticks or to corporal punishment, in order to ill-treat those who say such things to them. They also say and believe that when the soul of Christ descended into the underworld, in order not to be known, it clothed itself with divinity, just as when it was in the present life, so that it was not known, it clothed itself with its divinity in its body.

XXVI. Also, what the Armenians say and believe, that although the resurrection from death pertains only to the flesh, which had been dead, yet in Christ, because it was only the divine nature after the union, it did the works of the flesh and the works of the soul as it pleased, although in Christ neither there would be flesh and no soul after the union.

XXVII. Also, what the Armenians believe and hold, that the Lord rose at the sixth hour on the Sabbath after Parasceven; and they say that they have this from the tradition of Gregory, who was their ancient Catholicos, to whom, as they say, it was revealed when he was in the Lord's Sepulcher, that the Lord had risen at the sixth hour of the said Sabbath day. And so, it was determined among the Armenians; and at the said hour they celebrate the resurrection of the Lord; and later on the same day they eat eggs and cheese, but not meat. Now count the three days and nights during which the Lord was in the womb of the earth, because on the night following the fifth day, the Lord gave his body and blood to his disciples, who were on earth, they ate and drank his body and blood and thus buried Christ in themselves; and they count that night; and afterwards the following day until that hour, when on the day of Parasceves there was darkness over the whole earth, for the first day and night; but that time during which the said darkness lasted, they count as the second night; and they count the day which was after the said darkness as the second day; they count the night which precedes the Sabbath as the third night; and the Sabbath until noon for the third day; and they say that their aforesaid opinion was confirmed by the blessed Sylvester, the pope, at the instance of the said Gregory; and they believe more in the said opinion than in the gospels of Mark and Luke, who say that on the first Sabbath, that is, Sunday, the Lord rose again.

XXVIII. Also, that the Armenians do not know how to answer those things which are contained in the Gospels, where it is clearly written that after his resurrection Christ had a true human body, when they say that in the very union human nature was converted into divinity; except this only, that the divine will did according to what it willed, and showed that it had a human body, when yet it did not.

XXIX. Likewise, although according to the Armenians there was in Christ after the union only the divine nature, into which his human nature was converted, the Armenians still say and hold that the divine nature was subject to the will of

Christ, so that he could do with it what he willed. and thus, as they say, when his divine nature willed, he was mortal and also dead, and when he willed, he became immortal, as was done after his resurrection, taking to prove this what is said in John: I *live, and ye shall live.*

XXX. Likewise, the Armenians say and maintain that from the fact that Christ ascended into heaven, human nature ceased to exist in him after the union; otherwise, if the human nature had been in him after the union, he would not have ascended to heaven, but would have been transferred to an earthly paradise, as happened to Elijah and Enoch.

XXXI. Again, what the Armenians hold, that those authorities of the Prophets and Apostles: *Christ ascending on high, led the captive into captivity,* and that Christ robbed principalities and powers and transferred them to himself, do not mean that he did this when Christ ascended into heaven, but they understand when Christ, ascending from the underworld, brought with him the souls of men who were there and placed them in that earth or air until the day of judgment.

XXXII. Also, what the Armenians say and hold, that Christ, ascending to hell, bound the demons that were there and also on earth, so that they could not tempt or offend men as they did before; but it is now three hundred years since all the demons were loosed and seduced men from the faith of Christ throughout the whole world, with the exception of the Armenians; but for thirty years on this side those men of Lesser Armenia, and for twenty-five years on this side the Armenians of Greater Armenia, seduced them from the faith of Christ, because, as they say, from that time the Armenians put water in wine in the Sacrifice, and made the feast of the Nativity of the Lord on the twenty-fifth day of December, and so , seduced by demons, they abandoned the faith of Christ.

XXXIII. Likewise, what the Armenians say, and hold is that Christ had humanity after his ascension, but he had no human nature, no will, and no human activity. They also say and maintain that Christ, having ascended into heaven, did not come suddenly to the right hand of the Father, but on the tenth day after his ascension, and in the nine days which are from the day of his ascension until the day of Pentecost, Christ was among the angels, so that he was for one day on one order of angels and on another day on another and each order of angels celebrated him on one day; on the tenth day he reached the right hand of the Father and immediately sent the Holy Spirit to the apostles, and for this reason the Armenians celebrate those ten days.

XXXIV. Likewise, what the Armenians say and maintain about Greater Armenia is that they are a Catholic and apostolic Church and for this reason they have a Catholicos, and their Church is also apostolic, because they themselves hold to the faith that the Apostles preached. and for this reason, they are the Catholic and Apostolic Church. But the Greek Church is not a Catholic or Apostolic Church, because they put water in the wine in the Sacrifice, and because they say that there are two natures in Christ, and because they make the feast of the Nativity of the Lord on the twenty-fifth day of December. They also say and maintain that the Roman Church is not a Catholic and Apostolic Church, for the same reasons that they say about the Greek Church and also because it corrupted the Christian faith, by making and accepting the Council of Chalcedon at the instance of the blessed Pope Leo. They also say and maintain that the Roman and Greek churches will cease to exist before the general resurrection or at the time of Antichrist; but the church of the Armenians will last until the end; and that those of Lesser Armenia, with the exception of the king and some nobles, are of the Church of Greater Armenia and are worse than those of Greater Armenia, and do not want to receive any teacher unless he is from Greater Armenia. They also say that the king and nobles of Armenia Minor, because they hold the aforesaid articles with the Roman and Greek Church, do not belong to the Catholic and Apostolic Church.

XXXV. Likewise, the Armenians say and maintain that the Catholic Church was spread over the whole world from the beginning, because some of all nations believed in Christ; but afterwards in the Council of Chalcedon the faith of the Church was corrupted and destroyed, from the fact that it was determined there, that in Christ there were two natures and one person; and all who received the said council were the Catholic Church; and because the said

Armenians did not receive the said council, but condemned it, therefore the Catholic Church is only among them, with the exception of a few of the Church of Armenia Minor.

XXXVI. Likewise, what the Armenians believe, and hold is that there is only one Catholic Church with them, because, as they say, they have those things which make it one holy Church, namely, one baptism and one faith in Christ and one Holy Spirit and one God and Lord. which are not in the other Churches which are called Christian, because, as they say, the Armenians have true baptism, for which reason they rebaptize all who come to them from other Churches, nay, as they say, they baptize more truly, because they do not consider the baptism given in other Churches to be true baptism They also have, as they say, the true faith which the other churches destroyed by accepting the Council of Chalcedon. They also have the true Holy Spirit and the true God and Lord, which the other churches do not have, because they denied God and the Lord in the Council of Chalcedon, saying that in Christ there are two natures and one person. for which reason they do not simply say in the symbol: *And into one holy church;* but *into that holy church;* receiving this ly, for the church of the Armenians.

XXXVII. Also, that from the time of the emperor Heraclius on this side, there were three Catholicons in Armenia, holding different faiths and different baptisms from each other; for the Catholicos of Columba says that the Father and the Son and the Holy Spirit were crucified on the cross; and those who are subject to him baptize in water; But the middle Catholicos and his subjects say that the only Son of God was crucified on the cross; and for the greater part they baptize in water, yet a few baptize in wine, yet they do not immerse the baptized *in the name of the Father, and of the Son, and of the Holy Spirit;* but the third Catholicos has held for fifty years on this side what the church of the Greeks has held. Nevertheless, the said three Catholicon and their subjects agree in these, that in Christ there is one nature, just as one person, which is a divine nature; and that they do not put water in the wine in the Sacrifice, nor do they celebrate the Lord's Nativity on the twenty-fifth day of December, with the exception of the third Catholicos, who is separated from the first two on this side by fifty years; But every one of the said Catholicons says that he holds true faith and has true baptism, and that other Catholicons do not have true faith nor true baptism from him. and thus, because they are different from one another, there is not one Church among them, but one and another.

XXXVIII. Also, what the Armenians believe and hold, that in other Churches the remission of sins is not given by the Armenian Churches, because other churches denied the true faith by receiving the Council of Chalcedon; nor do they have true baptism, because they mix water with wine in the sacrifice, saying that the water which flowed from the side of Christ gives power to the sacrament of baptism alone; and therefore those churches which mix water with wine have lost baptism; for which reason the remission of sins does not take place among them, but takes place only in the church of the Armenians; and therefore the priests of the Armenians forbid their subjects not to receive the sacraments from others than from the Armenians, because others do not have those sacraments.

XXXIX. Likewise, what the Armenians say and hold is that the people subject to one Catholicos can receive the said sacraments from another Catholicos or his priests and the said sacraments are valid for the said people; but the bishops and priests of one Catholicos cannot receive the sacraments from another Catholicos or its subjects, and if they did receive such sacraments, they would not be valid for them.

XL. Also, the Armenians believe and hold that no Armenian can obtain the remission of sins through the bishops or priests of the Roman or Greek Church; but some of the Armenians say that remission of sins can be effected among the Armenians by the bishops and priests of the Armenians; but others say that the bishops or priests of the Armenians do nothing for the remission of sins, neither principally nor ministerially, but God alone forgives sins; nor are bishops or priests employed to make the so-called remission of sins, unless they themselves have received the power to speak from God; and therefore when they absolve they say: *God forgive you your sins* or: *I forgive you your sins on earth and God forgive you in heaven.*

XLI. Likewise, the Armenians say and hold that after someone has lost God's grace by sinning, he never again rises in equal grace.

XLII. Likewise, the Armenians say and hold that Christ's passion alone, without any other gift of God, even a gratifying one, is sufficient for the remission of sins. nor do they say that the gratifying or justifying grace of God is required for the remission of sins, nor that gratifying grace is given in the sacraments of the New Law.

XLIII. Likewise, the Armenians say and maintain that human free will is not sufficient for them to sin, but the devil makes and instigates men to sin; so that if there were no demons, no man would sin.

XLIV. Also, although the Armenians pray in the Mass and in other places for the attainment of both spiritual and temporal goods and for the removal of evils, they do not pray for the dead, that they may obtain repose in the present, but only in the future.

XLV. Likewise, among the Armenians, when one of them has died, such an observance takes place: that in the evening, clean animals according to the Law of Moses, such as sheep, goats, and oxen, covered with silken cloths, are brought to the door of the church; to which place the clerics of the said church go out and the priest blesses the salt and puts the blessed salt in the mouth of the said animals; and afterward the said animals are anointed with linseed oil; and then, after their blood has been shed, they are killed, and the clerics eat of the meat of the said animals the following night with salt; but the priest, who must celebrate in the crucifixion for the dead, does not eat of the flesh of the said animals until after the Mass. And they do the aforesaid, because they say and maintain that although the remission of sins is chiefly effected by the blood of Christ, yet the said remission of sins is not effected unless the blood of the aforesaid animals be shed, for the remission of the sins of the living and the dead, because the Law of Moses says that the remission of sins is by effusion the blood of unclean beasts, and without it there is no remission of the sins of the living and the dead; and the Lord says in the Gospel that he did not come to dissolve the law, but to fulfill it, which he would have dissolved if the remission of sins had been effected without the shedding of the blood of wild animals. And in this regard also Damascenus reproached them, saying that the said Armenians, receiving from the errors of the Jews, Saracens, heathens, and other erring men, formed their faith from those errors; and on the diet of faith in the council of Manesguerden they composed a book, which among them is called *the Root of Faith*.

XLVI. Also, that the said Armenians observe the discretion of the food of clean and unclean animals, according to what the law of Moses says; and although some of the Armenians eat pork, yet according to them, if the priest ate of the pig, he could not afterwards drive out demons from the besieged bodies, because, as they say, the Lord, driving out demons from two men, sent them into pigs.

XLVII. Likewise, when the Armenians fast on the days of fasting instituted among them, on the diet days they do not eat meat, fish, eggs, cheese, butter, milk, or oil. because they say that all these things are a kind of flesh; but they eat only herbs, bread, and wine; they may, however, eat as often as they like on the days on which they fast. They also say and preach that those who eat fish, eggs, cheese, butter, and oil during fasting days are cursed and infidels and set against the faith and are separated from Christ's flock.

XLVIII. Also, the Armenians say and hold that if Armenians commit any crime once, with some exceptions, their Church can absolve them as to the guilt and punishment of the said crimes, but if someone later commits the said crimes again, he could not be absolved by their Church.

XLIX. They also say that if one of them takes a first and second wife after baptism, he can be absolved by them, but if he takes a third or fourth and so on, he cannot be absolved by their church, because they say that such a marriage is fornication, and they consider such a heathen. so that they neither communicate with him at the end nor bring him out of their house to be buried through the gate of the house but break the wall of the house and bring out his body through an opening in the wall. They neither celebrate Mass nor bury him with an ecclesiastical burial but treat him as if he were a heathen. If, however, he who takes a third wife divorces her while he is alive, so that he does not return to her afterwards, they receive him for penance and impose on him fifteen years for penance, so that during the said years he shall not eat meat, fish, and the aforesaid dairy products; and if he completes the said penance and afterwards dies, they treat him as another Christian in life and in death.

L. Likewise, the Armenians say and hold that if someone has committed some external sin of carnal lust before receiving Holy Orders, he must confess the said sin to the confessor, and then the bishop who makes the Orders, asks the said confessor if he is worthy to be ordained; to which the priest replies that he does not; and thus he is rejected from receiving the Holy Order. But if, after being ordained, he commits such a sin of lust, he must, if he wishes to be absolved, confess to his confessor; and then that confessor deposes him from the execution of the Order; and if afterwards the acts of the said Order are executed, the said confessor says this to the bishop, even in the presence of others, and reveals to him in what or where he has sinned. Women also, with whom such men have sinned, boast of themselves, saying: *I have deposed such a priest;* from which it happens among the Armenians that there are many who do not want to confess the said sins while they live, lest they be repulsed from receiving the Sacred Orders; and if they have received them, they may not afterwards be removed from the execution of the Order.

LI. Also, what the Armenians say and hold is that these sins are unpardonable and their Church cannot forgive these sins, because Christ did not give the Church the power to forgive such sins, that is, if someone commits the sin of lust in the mouth of a man or woman and if he blasphemes Christ or the Christian faith or the cross; and they do not regard such blasphemers as Christians, nor do they administer the ecclesiastical sacraments to them, while they live, nor when they die, treat them as Christians, nor receive their children for baptism, unless they are converted and do penance.

LII. Also, what the said Armenians say and hold, that if a man once commits the sin of adultery, sodomy, bestiality, or murder, or apostasy from the faith, by making himself a Saracen or a Jew, and even if a man says that in Christ there are two natures and one person, he may be absolved by their Church, however, should not be communicated except at the end of their life. And if anyone commits the said sins or even other sins several times, he cannot be absolved by the Church, except the first time; and if, after he has once been confessed and absolved from any of the aforesaid sins, he commits the said sin again, the first absolution is invalid.

LIII. Likewise, what the said Armenians say and hold, that if a priest having a wife, when she commits sodomy, he does not sin, nor is he deposed if he confesses it, but in this he is left to his own conscience, whether he confesses or not, if he wishes.

LIV. Also, that among the Armenians Catholicons and bishops excommunicate Armenians as they please, without any fault of the excommunicated, and without any prior warning. And they say that those excommunicated by them cannot be absolved of any sin, except by the Catholicos or the bishops who excommunicated them; if, however, they go to another Catholicos or bishops, other Catholicos subject to them can be absolved from the said excommunication and from their sins. They also say and maintain that ecclesiastical sacraments should not be administered to the excommunicated. And if a person dies after being excommunicated, his friends go or send to him who excommunicated him and give him money or other things worth money, as they agree with him; and then, excommunicating him, he gives them permission to bury him in an ecclesiastical burial. Those who do for him those things which were said above about animals; yet they do not absolve him from excommunication in any other way.

LV. Likewise, the Armenians say and hold that the sentence of excommunication, even justly issued, according to the Lord's ordinance, because he does not want to obey the Church when warned, nor to make amends for the sin he has committed, does not cut him off from the kingdom of God, because just as well, the excommunicated as the not excommunicated goes to the kingdom of God; but fornication, adultery, murder, and if a priest takes a second wife, and if any of the Armenians say that in Christ there are two natures and two operations and one person, these exclude them from the kingdom of God and not excommunication issued because of disobedience to the Church; hence the Armenians consider excommunication to be of little or no value.

LVI. Also, what the Armenians say and hold, that if someone had been baptized in the Armenian Church and had subsequently fallen into heresy or apostasy from the faith, pretending to be a Muslim or a Jew and then wanted to return to the Armenian Church, he should not be rebaptized, but only anointed with chrism. nor is it absolved in any other way; It is imposed on him, however, that he should go to that place where he committed apostasy from the faith and there before everyone confess his sin and deny the perfidy he committed. If, however, a person had been baptized in the Church of some Catholicos of the Armenians and afterwards converted to the faith of the Roman Church or of the Greeks, if afterwards he wished to come to the first Church in which he had been first baptized, that Church should baptize him as if he had never been baptized, but had always been a Saracen or a heathen. . But if a person had first been baptized in the Roman or Greek Church and later wanted to come to the Armenian Church, that Church to which he came would baptize him as if he had never been baptized but had always been a heathen or a Saracen. And because the Armenians therefore say that those baptized in the Roman or Greek Church, when they come to the Church of the Armenians, they must be rebaptized, because the Roman and Greek Church, because they say that there are two natures in Christ, have denied the faith, and because they put water in the wine in the Sacrifice , they do not have water for baptism, because the water which flowed from the side of Christ can only serve the sacrament of baptism, hence when it is placed in the Sacrifice by the said churches, the same churches do not have water for baptism, without which baptism cannot take place. from this also the so-called churches do not have baptism, because they do not have true Chrism, without which true baptism is not given; and because of the aforesaid, that the Latin and Greek Churches do not have true baptism, but only the Armenian Church has the said true baptism, because it holds and has the opposites of the said Churches; and therefore the Armenian Church baptizes those baptized in the Latin or Greek Church, when they come to it.

LVII. Likewise, the Armenians say and maintain that the true chrism is made in this way, that they have different aromatic flowers and others that they can find on the day of Ramis-palms and they boil them in wine and then they take the said wine and for four days before the day of the Supper they put the said wine in oil and they boil it at the same time, and then many bishops and priests stand by, saying many prayers, while this decoction takes place. And then, on the day of the Supper, one vial of the said oil is taken, and in the same vial the Catholicos puts the balm, and afterwards the Catholicos celebrates Mass; and when the Catholicos raises the Corpus Christi, one of the bishops who stands by him raises the said flask and the Catholicos says the prayers. And then the said flask is placed in different vessels which stand there beside the altar, and thus the true chrism is made only by the Catholicos in the manner aforesaid; and without such chrism a true baptism cannot be given. Hence it happened among them that children brought for baptism, because the priest has no knowledge of the said chrism, or those who brought the child, do not want to give as much for chrism as the priest wanted, frequently die without baptism. of which children the Armenians say, that on the day of judgment they will be baptized of the blood which flowed from the side of Christ, because, as they say, when Christ was dying on the cross, the moon came down and received the blood of Christ, which still remains in the moon; and from this there appears something black in the moon, which was not visible before; and on the day of judgment the said blood will flow from the moon, from which the said little ones will be baptized, so that they may thus enter the <kingdom> of heaven.

LVIII. Also, what the Armenians say and hold, that for this to be a true baptism, these three things are required, namely, water, chrism made in the manner aforesaid, and the Eucharist; so that if someone were to baptize someone in water, saying: *I baptize you in the name of the Father, and of the Son, and of the Holy Spirit. Amen,* and afterwards he was not anointed with the said chrism, there would be no baptism. Even if the sacrament of the Eucharist had not been given to him, he would not have been baptized. And even among them children are not baptized before they are eight days old. And the species of the sacrament of the Eucharist are dissolved in water or wine and placed in the mouth of the first baptized, and thus they receive the sacrament of the Eucharist, and then they are said to be truly baptized. If these three things were not done, the Armenians would not consider the child truly baptized. They also say that children are not baptized for the remission of sins, because they have no sin; but adults are baptized for the remission of sins, not because they are baptized in water, but because they are anointed with the said chrism and receive the sacrament of the Eucharist.

LIX. Also, that the Armenians baptize in different ways, both as to the material and as to the form of baptism. As for the material, because some, though few, baptize in pure wine, others in milk, and others generally in water. But as to the form, there is no certain form of baptism among them, but each bishop or priest arranges for himself the form in which to baptize, and the manner of baptizing he chooses. For some of them, who baptize in water, do not name, while baptizing, the three divine persons, saying: *Let him be baptized in the name of the Father, and of the Son, and of the Holy Spirit;* but while they are washing the baptized in water, they say the gospel from that place: *Jesus came from Galilee to the Jordan to John* , even to that place: *and a voice was heard saying: This is my Son.* But others, while washing the baptized, say: *The voice of the Lord over the waters; The God of majesty thundered; Lord over many waters.* Others, however, while washing the baptized, say an antiphon, namely: ' *While the apostles were in the upper room, suddenly there came a sound from heaven like a violent spirit with a loud voice and set them on fire without burning.* They also say another antiphon: *Suddenly the Holy Spirit descended in the likeness of glory upon the Apostles;* and another also, which is as follows: *'Blessing on high of the Holy Spirit proceeding from the Father, through whom the Apostles were intoxicated with immortal wine and invited the earth to heaven '.* But those who baptize in wine, while they wash him who is being baptized, say: ' *I wash you in wine, that you may be strong and not suffer the cold.'* As for those who baptize in milk, no form is expressed. But others, while they are washing those to be baptized, say that they themselves would like to commit indecency with the mother of the child who is being baptized. Some of the Armenians also, when they place the person to be baptized in water, say: ' *Let such a one be baptized in the name of the Father, and of the Son, and of the Holy Spirit* .' and then, when they draw out of the water, they say the same words; and then they anoint the baptized with chrism in the eyes, in the ears, in the forehead, in the nose, in the mouth, in and under the armpits, on the knee and under the knee, on the feet, on the soles, saying certain words, and afterwards they share the baptized from the sacrifice of the altar. And so, as they say, a man is truly and fully baptized and not otherwise.

LX. Also, that if an Armenian is baptized in water, wine, or milk in the aforesaid ways, even if, while being baptized in water, it is said: *Let him be baptized in the name of the Father and of the Son and of the Holy Spirit,* let him pass over to the Latin or Greek Church and afterwards return to the first Church. he is thus rebaptized as if he had always been a heathen; If, however, a Catholic passes from the church of one Catholic to the church of another Catholic, that Catholic to whose church he goes makes him deny the faith of that Catholic who baptized him and chrismated him in the manner aforesaid, saying that the chrism of another Catholic is worth nothing but his own; however, he does not rebaptize him, with the exception of the Catholicos of Armenia Minor, who rebaptizes and chrismates those baptized and chrismated in the churches of the Catholicos of Greater Armenia coming to the church of Armenia Minor, in the manner aforesaid.

LXI. Likewise, the Armenians say that by virtue of the sacrament of baptism, one who is baptized becomes a member of the Church and can participate in the Sacraments and becomes a Christian, and after the final judgment, unless otherwise prevented, he will enter the kingdom of heaven.

LXII. Likewise, the Armenians say and maintain that although it is said in their ancient Ordinariate that the remission of sins is given through baptism, yet they themselves have explained this in this way, that this has no truth in regard to children who are baptized in their infancy under the age of twelve years, because they regard such as innocent and without sin; because the Armenians themselves consider the sin of lust to be the greatest sin, which such children cannot commit; but of those who are baptized after having committed sins of lust, they say that such are baptized for the remission of sins. The so-called Armenians also hold that those who have not committed the sin of lust are virgins and innocent, even if they had departed unbaptized.

LXIII. Likewise, among the Armenians of both Armenia the Sacrament of Confirmation is not given, because as they say, those who preached faith to them from the beginning did not give them such a Sacrament; and although the Apostles sent Peter and John to those who had been baptized in Samaria by Philip, to lay hands on them and receive the Holy Spirit, which seems to belong to the Sacrament of Confirmation, yet the Armenians say that those who had been baptized by Philip had not received the truth baptism, because Philip was only a deacon and not a priest or a bishop, because only a priest and a bishop can give true baptism; and therefore the said two apostles were sent to them, that they might receive the true baptism and the Holy Spirit. The said Armenians also say that the eunuch baptized by Philip did not receive the Holy Spirit in such a baptism, but after Philip had been taken away from him, the Holy Spirit came upon the eunuch.

LXIV. Likewise, the Catholicos of Armenia Minor says that the Sacrament of Confirmation is worth nothing, and if it is worth something, he himself gave permission to his priests to confer the same Sacrament.

LXV. Likewise, the Armenians say and hold that the anointing made with chrism in the nine places mentioned above is valid for Christians as long as they live, instead of all the anointings that are done through the Latin Church. hence with them there is no Sacrament of Confirmation or Extreme Anointing, nor, when priests or bishops are consecrated, are their hands or heads anointed; but when bishops or priests are dead, they are carried before the altar, and there their heads and foreheads and right hands are anointed, and then the people come and kiss the right hand of the aforementioned and make their offerings as if they were celebrating the first Mass. and afterwards clean animals covered with silken cloths are brought to the door of the church and killed in the manner aforesaid and afterwards eaten.

LXVI. Likewise, all the Armenians commonly say and hold that by these words placed in their Canon of the Mass, when they are said by the priest; He *took the bread giving thanks, broke it, gave it to his holy chosen and reclining disciples, saying: Take and eat from this all: This is my body, which is distributed for you and for many, for the remission of sins. Similarly, taking the cup, he blessed and broke it, gave thanks, drank it, and gave it to his chosen saints and reclining disciples, saying: Take, drink from this, all of you: This is my blood of the new testament, which is poured out for you and for many, for the remission of* sins nor do they themselves intend to make the Body and Blood of Christ, but they only say the said words recitatively, that is, by reciting what the Lord did when he instituted the Sacrament. And after the said words the priest says many prayers placed in their Canon and after the said prayers he comes to the place where it is said in their Canon: ' *We worship, we pray and we ask you, kind God, send in us and for this purpose the essential gift of your Spirit Holy, through which bread you will truly make the blessed Body of our Lord and Savior Jesus Christ* . And the priest says these words three times. Then the priest says over the cup and the blessed wine: ' *Truly you will become the blood of our Lord and Savior Jesus Christ* '; and by these words they believe that the Body and Blood of Christ are made. The so-called Armenians also have a different rite in celebrating Mass, because some of them place two cups on the altar, in which they put bread and wine; and some put only one in which they put the wine; and their cups are either earthen or wooden. And some celebrate Mass in common clothes, and some are dressed in sacred clothes; and some celebrate with the people present and some with the people excluded and the doors closed. The priest, celebrating, enters and leaves the church alone and does not show the Lord's body to the people at all. and it is still done in several places in this way, that they celebrate under closed doors, until the priest says: *Look;* namely, when he lifts up the sacrament, that the people may see; and then the doors of the church are opened.

LXVII. Likewise, the Armenians do not say that after the said words of consecration of the bread and wine the transubstantiation of the bread and wine took place into the true Body and Blood of Christ, which was born of the Virgin Mary and suffered and rose again, but they hold that that sacrament is a model or similitude or the figure of the true Body and Blood of the Lord; and this was specially said by some of the teachers of the Armenians, to wit, that there was not the true Body and Blood of Christ, but the model and similitude thereof. They also say that when Christ instituted the Sacrament, he did not transubstantiate the bread and wine into his body and blood, but only instituted the model and likeness of his body and blood. for which reason they do not call the sacrament of the altar the body and blood of the Lord, but *a sacrifice* or *sacrifice* or *communion*. A certain teacher also called Narces has expressed in his books that when the priest says these words: ' *This is my body* ' then the dead body of Christ is there; but when the priest says: *Through whom* , as it is intended, there is the living body of Christ; He did not, however, express whether the real body of Christ was there, or a similitude of it. And that the Armenians also explain what is stated in their Canon of the Mass: ' *Through whom the blessed bread is made the true body of Christ* ', thus *the true body of Christ,* because there is made a true likeness and model of the body and blood of Christ. Hence Damascenus, criticizing them for this, said that it was two hundred years ago, that the Armenians had lost all the Sacraments, and that those Sacraments which they had, had not been handed down to them by the Apostles, or by the Greek or Latin Church, but they had confined the Sacraments to themselves, as they wished.

LXVIII. Likewise, the Armenians say and hold that if an ordained priest or bishop commits fornication, even in secret, he loses the power to administer and administer all the Sacraments that belong to the bishop or priest; and such sacraments performed by them have no efficacy or power. But if it were public that they were fornicators, no Armenian would receive the Sacraments made by them, because they believe that such Sacraments have no power or efficacy, because such fornicators have lost the power to make and administer the Sacraments; they say, however, that a good layman and faithful person who has received the Eucharist through a bishop or a priest who has the power to administer the Sacrament of the Eucharist can minister it to others.

LXIX. Likewise, the said Armenians say that if a bishop or priest commits fornication or any other kind of lasciviousness, secretly or publicly, he loses the power to administer and administer the Sacraments that belong to him; but if he becomes a heretic or apostates from the faith, as if he becomes a Muslim or a Jew, or commits any other crime, such as murder, perjury, and so on, he does not lose the said power of making and administering the Sacraments, but it is sufficient that he repent of such sins, whether said He has committed sins publicly or secretly.

LXX. Likewise, the Armenians do not say or hold that the sacrament of the Eucharist, received worthily, works in receiving the remission of sins or the relaxation of the punishment due to sin, or that through it the grace of God is given or its increase, but they only say that these are the effects of the Sacrament of the Eucharist, namely that he who receives this Sacrament, Christ remains in it, because the Body of Christ enters into his body and is converted into him, just as other foods are converted into what is nourished. And because the Eucharist remains in the receiver, they say that the priest who receives the Body of Christ must not be phlebotomized afterwards for three days; and because a priest did the opposite, blood and fire came out of the phlebotomy. The Armenians also say that the effects of the Eucharist are to guard against lightning and hail, and from other noxious influences of the air, and from infirmities of the body, and such bodily ills of themselves or of their loved ones. And they say the same thing with regard to these corporal punishments of the Sacrament of Penance, because of course men are protected from such punishments by the said Sacrament.

LXXI. Also, that it is six hundred and twelve years since the aforesaid council was celebrated by the Armenians in the city of Manesguerden, and there the patriarch of the Syrians, the Catholicos, the bishops and the teachers of the Armenians determined that in the Sacrifice of the altar water should not be mixed with wine; and nevertheless they determined there that those who mix water with wine in the sacrament of the altar do not have true baptism, because that water which flowed from the side of Christ on the cross can only serve the sacrament of baptism. and therefore, those who put water in wine have lost the sacrament of baptism. They also determined in the said council that if water were placed in the sacrifice of the altar, that there would be no Sacrament, because the Lord said after the preparation of the Sacrament of the Eucharist: *I will not drink from this seed of the vine,* and thus, only the seed of the vine should be placed in the sacrifice and not the water. In which council they also anathematized those who put or would put water in the said sacrifice; and they detest this so much, that if a Mass is celebrated in any Armenian church, in which water is mixed with wine, some part of the roof of the church is opened, so that the rays of the sun may enter it, by the entrance of which the consecration of the said church is removed, and afterwards before any

Armenian in the diet for the church to celebrate Mass, it is necessary that the said church be reconciled.

XXLII. Likewise, the ancient Armenians said and held that no one who was not ordained a priest, no matter how good his life, could perform the Sacrament of the Eucharist; and that those who were ordained as priests, if they were of bad life, could not perform the said Sacrament; but good priests could do this and not others. But modern Armenians say that good and bad priests, as long as they have not abandoned the law of the Armenians, nor have they conformed to the law of the Latin or Greek Church, nor have they committed the sins mentioned above, can perform the said Sacrament. But those priests who have rejected the law of the Armenians or have become followers of the law of the Greek or Latin Church, because by rejecting it they have become heretics, cannot perform the said Sacrament.

LXXIII. Likewise, the Armenians have a certain canon that if someone had been baptized in any of the churches that held that in Christ there are two natures and one person and he wanted to receive the Sacrament of the Eucharist from the Armenian priests, the same sacrament would not be given to him by the said priests, unless he first denied baptism that he had previously accepted and cursed those who say that there are two natures in Christ and who mix water with wine in the Sacrifice; having done this, they rebaptize him in the Armenian manner, and then give him the Sacrament of the Eucharist completed by them in the Armenian manner; and that the Armenian priests, while they celebrate Mass with the doors of the church closed, according to what has been said above, curse those who say that there are two natures in Christ and who mix water in the Sacrifice and who do any reverence to the images of God or the Saints.

LXXIV. Also, that among the Armenians of Greater Armenia there is no image of the Crucifix, nor are any other images of the Saints held.

LXXV. Likewise, that a certain teacher of the Armenians, when he had come to a certain place where the solemnity was being celebrated and the priest had lifted up the Sacrament of the Eucharist, so that it could be seen by the people, the said teacher cursed the same priest, saying that the mystery of the faith ought to be kept in secret and not to be shown to the people, and that by showing the said Sacrament, the priest can be seen saying to the people: 'Do not be afraid, because this sacrament is one piece of bread.'

LXXVI. Likewise, that there were three Armenians in Bononia, who had first been baptized in the form of the Armenians, and afterwards had been baptized in the form of the Latin Church (under the condition, of course, that they had not been properly washed by baptism, as is evident from the papal letters), who, when men afterwards came to Florence, while the Armenians asked them whether they had bathed, calling bathing a baptism received in the Latin Church; who, when they had answered them that they were, told them that they should deny the aforesaid bathing. When they would not do this, they beat them so much that one of them died after a few days; but they kept the other two in prison for so long, until they denied the said bathing, saying that they considered the said bathing as if one dog had licked them; and they were, as is believed, rebaptized by them according to the manner of the Armenians; otherwise they would not give such people the Sacrament of the Eucharist even at the end, no matter how much they asked.

LXXVII. Likewise, when certain Armenian clerics and laymen had been baptized in the form of the Latin Church, the Catholicos of Armenia Minor caused them to be arrested and dishonored, by completely shaving their heads and half of their beards and tearing their clothes and then putting them in prison and forcing them to receive the Sacrament of Baptism in the form of the Roman Church, to deny; and because they would not do it, he caused them to be kept in prison for a long time.

LXXVIII. Also, that when two archbishops, doubting whether they were really ordained and baptized by the Armenians, had come to the Catholicos who is now of Minor Armenia, the said Catholicos called the aforesaid archbishops and forbade them this: first, that they should not celebrate the Latin Mass, but the ancient Mass of the Armenians; secondly, he commanded them that they should not observe the fasts of the Roman Church, but the ancient fasts of the

Armenians; thirdly, he ordered that they should not baptize anyone who doubted his baptism and came to them to ask for true baptism, but that they should tell them that the baptism of the Armenians is better than the baptism of the Roman Church; fourthly, he prevented them from making their people of the Armenians Latin, because that so-called Catholicos said that it was better that his people should go to hell like the Armenians, than that they should become Latins and all go to paradise; fifthly, he ordered them not to teach the Armenian children either the Latin language or the Latin letter, because when they learned the Latin letter, they would lose the language of the Armenians. And for the testimony and confirmation of these sayings is this, that in the same year the aforesaid Catholicos consecrated six Armenian bishops and received from them a public letter, that they would not give children from their parts to learn the Latin letter, nor send any Latin preacher to preach the truth of the Holy Roman Churches in their diocese and province. Likewise, any bishop whom he consecrates, he causes to anathematize those Armenians who wish to become true Catholics and obedient to the Roman Church. Sixthly, he forbade them that they should not preach that the Roman pope was the head of the Church in the Eastern parts, but he himself says and makes himself pope in the Eastern parts from the end of the sea to the great empire of the Tartars. And wisdom spoke many other inconvenient words and errors, and the said Catholicos restrained them all; and because they refused to obey him in the aforesaid, he made a severe persecution against them, for which reason one of them, after a year and a half, went to the island of Cyprus, and there he heard that the said Catholicos, with the consent of the king of Armenia, had baptized or ordained those whom he and some other Latins had baptized or ordained under the condition in the form of the Roman Church, he made prisoners and degraded some of their priests, and put them in the hard prison of the king; but he imprisoned others, and they are still imprisoned, and their goods and possessions were confiscated and sold to others.

LXXIX. Also, that the priests and bishops of the Armenians impose penance on those Armenians who come to be baptized in the Greek or Latin Church, for some years, so that they may fast in the manner of the Armenians. Now the method is such that during the said time they must not eat meat, fish, milk, cheese, or eggs; they may, however, eat as many times as they like during the day. As for those Armenians who receive the Sacrament of the Eucharist in the

Greek or Latin Church, they impose a penance of five years, namely that they fast during the period in the manner mentioned above.

LXXX. Also, that among the Armenians during Lent, which they begin on the fiftieth Sunday, Mass is not celebrated in the churches, except on the Sabbath and Sunday; nor is it said of the other weeks of the year in which the Armenians fast. And they celebrate more Masses on the Sabbath day than on the other days mentioned at the times, because in common they celebrate all the feasts that come during the week on the Sabbath day, except the feasts of the Assumption of the Blessed Virgin Mary and the Exaltation of the Holy Cross, which feasts they celebrate on Sunday. But at another time of the year, they generally do not celebrate in the churches except on the said two days in the week, and then also they bring the animals to the door of the church and kill them in the manner aforesaid.

LXXXI. Also, that among the Armenians the people do not communicate except on the eve of the Epiphany and on the day of the Epiphany; so that those who have fasted for a week before the said vigil, take communion on the said vigil, or on the following night; and there they anathematize all those who make the feast of the Nativity of the Lord on the 25th day of December. On the following day, however, they make the feast of the Epiphany, and then those of the people who wish, communicate; even those who did not fast the said week; some also take communion on the day of the Lord's Supper and on the holy Sabbath.

LXXXII. Likewise, when some people must communicate through a priest, a general confession is made, stating the types of sins, not going down to any particular sin. and afterwards the people repeat the said confession; in secret, however, rarely or never does an Armenian confess his sins to a priest; and if he confesses, he does not say that he committed this or that particular sin, but says that the devil committed the said sin, or that he committed the said sin at the suggestion of another man. Now they allow themselves to confess their sins secretly and individually, because the priests would reveal their sins and impose on them very serious penances. for which reason the Armenians generally do not confess their sins except in general. And when the general confession has been said by the people, the priest says either: *'I forgive you your sins'* or: *God forgive you'*; and some say: *I forgive you your sins on earth, and God forgives you in heaven.* And the said priests say that unless they have completed the said penances, they must not share in the present life, nor will they enter into the kingdom of God; and they will be excluded from the grace and blessing of God. And among the Armenians priests and priests have no definite form of absolving their subjects from their sins. Also, what the said Armenians say and hold, that the said general confession is sufficient for the remission of sins and absolution; nor is it necessary that anyone should confess his sins to the priest in secret and in private; the said general absolution also applies to the absolution of sins, even if the transgression had not preceded it.

LXXXIII. Likewise, the seriously ill Armenians, when it is told to them that they are nearing death, they or their friends ask for communion and have it carried; and sometimes it happens that when they are very weak, the priests put communion in their mouths; and when they are very close to death, the priests make the sign of the cross over their mouths for communion, and thus bring communion back.

LXXXIV. Likewise, the Armenians say and hold that the Catholicos, the bishops, and the priest of the Armenians have the same and equal power to bind or loose, as much and as the Apostle Peter had, to whom it was said by the Lord: ' *Whatever you bind on earth shall be bound in heaven. and whatever you loose on earth will be loosed in heaven too;* and in this respect the priests of the Armenians have no less power than their Catholicoss and bishops.

LXXXV. Likewise, the Armenians say and hold that until the Council of Nicaea the Roman Pontiff had no greater power than the other patriarchs; but then it was determined by the will of the said council that the said Roman Pontiff should have power over the other patriarchs. What power did the Roman Pontiffs have until the Council of Chalcedon? But because in the said council, at the instance of when Pope Leo assembled, it was determined that in Christ there were two natures and one person, the Roman Pontiffs lost the said power and all those who consented to the said council; and from that time that full power of binding or loosing, which Christ of the Church in person blessed

Peter had contributed, he remained with the Armenians alone; and this also the Armenians determined in the aforesaid council of Manesguerdens, which was assembled there at the command of a certain Saracen, the nephew of Mahomet.

LXXXVI. Also, the Armenians say and maintain that after the Council of Chalcedon the Roman Pontiff does not enjoy more power over his subjects than he who presides over the Nestorians over the Nestorians or he who presides over the Greeks over the Greeks. They say even further that the pope knows what he can do, and the Armenians know what they can do.

LXXXVII. Also, that the king of the Armenians asked the Catholicos of Armenia Minor, whether if the pope excommunicated him, he would consider himself excommunicated, who answered that he did not, because the pope had nothing to do with him, nor had he himself received anything from the pope. The king, however, told him that if the pope ordered him to depose the said Catholicos, he would depose him himself.

LXXXVIII. Likewise, the Catholicons of the Armenians are elected, instituted and confirmed in this way, and receive the power pertaining to the Catholicos, and are deposed and otherwise punished; because the Catholicos of Columba and the Catholicos of Dehactamar choose any one of their own people whom they want and afterwards consecrate him as Catholicos; yet he does not use this power until the Catholicos who elected him is dead. Now after the said first Catholicos has died, the next Catholicos goes to the emperor of the Tartars, who is a heathen, and is confirmed by him as a Catholicos; and in order to be confirmed by him, money is required from him, as much as he can pay. This method of electing and confirming Catholicons was introduced into the Church of Greater Armenia by Sapor, king of the Persians, a heathen who worshiped fire and continues to this day. With this confirmation made by the said king, the same king gives his letters, that the bishops and subjects obey him, because he is confirmed by him; and that they give him certain sums of money, and afterwards other yearly; and all the priests give him the value of at least one florin annually, and for every deed of Christians and subjects he has the annual value of at least six large pieces of silver. and the said Catholicos has to pay to the said king every year a certain sum of money, which if he does not pay or commits another crime, the said king deposes him and punishes him even to death according to the amount of the crime committed by him. But the Catholicos of Armenia Minor is made in this way: because after the death of the Catholicos, the king of Armenia summons the bishops he wants, and they elect three bishops of Armenia Minor to the Catholicos and present them to the king. which king bows his knees before any of the aforesaid elect; and then that one of the elect, who has given more money to the king, is appointed by the king a Catholicos, and is confirmed by the fact that the king puts a ring on the finger of his hand. And this Catholicos, who is now, gave to the said king fifty thousand grosses, or their value, for his confirmation, and every year he gives him twenty thousand grosses, or their value. Now the said king can depose the said Catholicos and punish in other ways, whenever he pleases; and among the Catholic Armenians, the bishops and priests do not give any Order to anyone, except by intervening money, nor chrism, nor any other Sacrament, but all such things are venial with them.

LXXXIX. Likewise, the emperor of Greater Armenia, when he confirms the said Catholics, says to them: ' *Go and do the duty according to your faith, and we command that you may bless and curse and bind and release, according to your faith, as it shall appear to you, and we want that Christians who they are under you, let them obey you, and if they do not want to obey, we want those who are in charge of the herds to compel or punish them,* and he gives him the privilege of this. And in the same way the king of Greater Armenia becomes the Catholicos of Lesser Armenia, and the king of Lesser Armenia elects bishops and priests, receiving money from them; and afterwards he sends those chosen as bishops to the Catholicos, that they may be consecrated by him, and the priests to the bishops, that they may be ordained by them; who also bishops and priests are ordained by the Catholicos and by the bishops for money. And by the very fact that they are consecrated or ordained, immediately after consecration they receive from God a power to bind and loose similar to that which Christ gave blessed Peter the Apostle; and priests have as much power as bishops and catholicons.

XC. Likewise, the Armenians say and hold that the power which Christ gave blessed To Peter, saying to him, '*Whatsoever thou hast bound upon the earth, etc.*' are given only to the person of Peter, and for him alone, so that this power did not pass to any of his successors.

XCI. Also, what the Armenians say and hold, that the general power over the whole Church of Christ was not given blessed Peter and his successors were not given power by Christ, but power was given to them by the Council of Nicaea, which power Peter's successors later lost.

XCII. Also, that among the Armenians there are only three Orders, namely, the acolyte, the deaconate, and the presbyterate; which orders are conferred on the bishop by money promised or received. And in the same way the said Orders of presbyterate and deaconate are confirmed, that is, by the laying on of hands, by saying certain words, with this only change, that in the ordination of a deacon the Order of the diaconate is expressed, and in the ordination of a priest the Order of the presbyterate. But no bishop among them can ordain another bishop, except a catholicos, who holds the Catholicos close to the pontifical, where the manner of consecrating a bishop is contained. But the said Catholicos consecrates no one as a bishop, unless money is given or promised, according to the means of consecration as a bishop or the value of the episcopate. And in Greater Armenia consecrating bishops, priests, deacons, or acolytes, they stand in common clothes, while they do the aforesaid and also during the ordination.

XCIII. Also, that when a man is ordained a deacon, the bishop gives him permission to contract marriage with a virgin; by which marriage he contracts, he ministers in the said Order and can also be promoted to the priesthood if he is married; but if an existing deacon takes a second wife, he is not afterwards promoted to the priesthood.

XCIV. Likewise, in Greater Armenia, when someone is ordained as a deacon, he is not given a book of the gospels or a robe under a certain form of words; nor, when a man is ordained a priest, is he given a cup with wine and a plate with bread under a certain form of words, which the Roman Church uses; nor are his hands anointed; nor, when a man is ordained a bishop, is the book of the gospels placed on his neck and shoulders; Neither his head nor his hands are anointed with chrism, as is done in the Roman Church. Even the Catholicos of Greater Armenia alone consecrates bishops, without other bishops assisting them.

XCV. Likewise, the Catholicos of Armenia Minor gave a certain authority to a certain priest, so that he could ordain as deacons whom he pleased among his subjects, whereas, among the Armenians of Greater Armenia, no one can ordain any deacon or priest, except the bishop alone.

XCVI. Likewise, the Catholicos of Armenia Minor, when he wants to consecrate bishops, puts on sacred clothes; yet he alone makes the said consecration; even if some bishops are present there for his honor, they do not consecrate the bishop with him, but only assist in the Mass when the Catholicos celebrates, just as the cardinals celebrate when the pope celebrates. they neither hold the pontifical book nor say the prayers which are said by the bishops assisting at the consecration of bishops.

XCVII. Also, that the Catholicos of the Armenians agree with the bishops subject to them, who do not come by succession, about a certain amount of money to be given to him annually; but if they do not pay, he deposes them and consecrates another bishop in his place, and with his letters writes to his people that he himself deposed the first bishop and appointed another; from which it happens that frequently for such a reason there are three or four bishops living together in one episcopate. He also restored the bishops deposited by him to their episcopates, if they would pay him the money about which they had agreed with him. But those bishops who come by succession, when they do not pay him the money, about which the said Catholicos agrees with them, he excommunicates them and does not give them chrism until they pay him the said money.

XCVIII. Likewise, the Catholicos of Armenia Minor holds with him the cubit of his arm and his hand still intact blessed Gregory, who was a Catholicos and was ordained a bishop after the manner of the Greek Church; what cubit and hand does the said Catholicos place upon the head and hands of those whom he ordained as bishops; and he says that if the imposition of the said hands and arms had not taken place on the head and hands of those who are ordained as bishops by him, they would not have been ordained as bishops, because the imposition of the said arms and hands constitute the consecrations of bishops. and for this reason he does not accept as bishops any bishops who were ordained by other Catholicons of Greater Armenia, because no other Catholicon, except himself, has the said arm and hand of Gregory.

XCIX. Also, that the Armenian bishops, coming to Italy, say that they were expelled from their episcopates by the Saracens; when, however, this is not true; and they say that they are archbishops, when, however, there is no archbishop in Armenia; for this, that they may sell the episcopacy to religious beggars for money; and many of them spent great sums of money in this way, and made many bishops in this way; and in the Roman Curia they also ordained many priests and deacons, without the permission of the dioceses in whose dioceses they lived; and for money. And they persecuted and persecute those Armenians who are baptized according to the rite of the Roman Church and those who hold the faith of the Roman Church; and they say that the Roman Church errs, but the Armenians themselves hold a good and correct faith.

C. Also, that among the Armenians there is no definite form of words expressing the matrimonial agreement between husband and wife; indeed, many are compelled by their parents and friends to come to the church, so that a marriage may take place between them; and although one or both of them say that they do not want to be joined together in matrimony, yet the marriage takes place between them in the presence of the church.

CI. Also, that among the Armenians the degrees of consanguinity and affinity, which among them is regarded as the same, are observed up to the seventh degree; If, however, some people, existing in the third degree and below, contract marriage with each other, they are allowed to stand in such marriage and are not troubled about this by the bishops.

CII. Also, that among the Armenians, if, after the marriage has been contracted, even carnal coupling has followed and children have been received, the wife does not please the husband; or on the contrary, the one who does not like the other spouse, or both, if they do not like each other, goes or goes to the bishop or priest and given money and according to what they agree between them, the bishop or priest separates the said marriage and gives permission to the other to marry, also with another spouse unwillingly; and this happens many times among the Armenians.

CIII. Also, among the Armenians there are many who have many wives at the same time, because men having wives in one place, when they are transferred to other places for the sake of trade or otherwise, take other wives in the said places to which they have transferred. Even in their own places there are many who have two wives living together, of whom they take one after the other, even making such marriages in the face of the church. Even among them spurious people succeed in the inheritance as if they were legitimate; and they shall be promoted without any other dispensation to all the Orders and to the episcopate and even to the state of Catholicon, as is the case with the nephew of Zacharias, who was the son of the concubine of the brother of the said Zacharias, who was promoted to the bishopric after his uncle.

CIV. Likewise, since the Armenians say that in the union itself human nature was transformed into divinity in Christ, the said Armenians say and believe that Christ will appear and judge in the judgment in divine form and not in human form.

CV. Likewise, the Armenians say and hold that after the General Judgment the just and the wicked will live forever, because from then on they will not die; They say, however, that some of the just men will go to the heavenly paradise after the Judgment, and others to the earthly paradise, and others to this earth, as was said above. in which places they will bear no punishment. They say, however, that eternal life, even in those who will go to the heavenly paradise, does not consist in the facial vision and enjoyment of God, because the essence of God will never be seen by any creature, but only his brightness.

CVI. Likewise, a certain Armenian Catholicon said and wrote that in the general resurrection all men will rise with their bodies, but still there will be no discrimination of the sexes in their bodies, because if there were such a discrimination of the sexes among them, then men would take wives and women would marry; the opposite of which the Lord says; but men and women will rise again with their bodies in another form, in which there will be no discrimination of the sexes.

CVII. Likewise, the Armenians hold that if someone is in danger of dying and does not have time to receive Communion, what they do is to make a cross with their hand on the ground, and from each arm of the said cross they take a little of the ground and eat it; and this eating of the earth is regarded by them as communion.

CVIII. Also, some great men of the Armenian laity have said, that as beasts expire in death, and so die, so also men; and as beasts, when they have been once dead, never rise again, so also men, after they have died, never rise again.

CIX. Likewise, among the Armenians, no one is punished for any error he holds.

CX. Also, that among the Armenians there are many other errors from the aforesaid, which errors are contained in the underwritten books of the Armenians, the first of which is entitled *Tenophacer*, that is, *Against the Festivities* which the Roman and Greek Churches celebrate. The second book is called *Anadoarmat,* that is, *the Root of Faith.* The third book is called *John of Mandagon.* The fourth book is called *John of Ossinensis.* The fifth book is called *Myascosutum,* that is, *One Speech.* The book is called *Michael the Patriarch of Antioch.* The seventh book is called *Paul of Taron.* The eighth book is entitled *Octavensis.* The ninth book is called *Matthew.* The tenth book is called *the Book of the Canons of the Apostles,* in which are contained all the errors of the Armenians. The eleventh book is called *Sergniz.* The twelfth book is called *Marocha,* from the name of the teacher who was so called; in which book the Gospels are expounded. The thirteenth book is called *Nanam,* in which the gospel of John is explained. The fourteenth is called *Ignatius*, in which the Gospel of Luke is expounded. The fifth and tenth are called *Ganazan*, that is, *the Book of Wands*. The sixteenth is called *Neguig pataracum*, in which the Mass is expounded. The seventeenth is called *Textorquire*, that is, *the Book of Letters*. The eighteenth is called *Aismanorc*, that is *Martyrology*. And that there are many other books of the Armenians, in which many errors are contained.

CXI. Also, the Armenians say that Christ did not put down the superfluities of nature, and, as they say, the reason is because the corruption of such superfluities is the generation of sins. And because Christ did not commit sins, therefore such corruption did not dominate him.

CXII. Likewise, they say that although Christ was circumcised according to the Law, yet his foreskin was not amputated, because it was not permissible to amputate anything from a deified body; and especially because it had been so ordained, that the first-born should be circumcised by cutting the foreskin and removing nothing; and Christ was the firstborn.

CXIII. They also say that God was defeated because of the love of man, because in his threats he was not found to be true, but partial; because he had told the man that he would die if he ate the forbidden fruit, and yet he was not completely dead after eating the fruit, because his soul was never dead. Again, he did not die in the body until the ninety-thirtieth year. Again, because all the animals did not rebel against him, but remained necessary in his service.

CXIV. They also say that God set a sign not to kill Cain, and it was so literally, because according to them no one killed him, but he submitted himself from the precipice. From this they infer that the Book of Genesis is false in regard to this, which seems to say that Lamech killed Cain.

CXV. Also, that when two bishops suffered severe persecutions from the Catholicon of Armenia Minor, of whose persecution mention was made above, they wrote a petition which they sent to the king, beseeching him to cause the said Catholicon to cease from the aforesaid persecution; And the same king answered them, that they themselves were in his power, and could not go out of his parts, either by sea or by land, unless they should go to the said catholicon, and pay him reverence, and be reconciled to him, and be subject to him in all things, and give a public letter concerning this, which the said Catholicon would ask of them; saying that the king himself was appointed by the Armenians and not by the Latins, and as long as he lived he had to work for the faith of the Armenian Church and honor the Catholicon of the Armenians, because he was its head. Now the letter which the said Catholicon requested from them was to contain the following, that they should honor the holy church of the Armenians and preach its faith and obey him as the Catholicon of the Armenians and acknowledge that he is their only head instead of God. and that they should not baptize any and honor the chrism of the Armenians, because that alone is the true chrism; and that all that he himself taught concerning the holy church of the Armenians and the rules, they should honor as the commandments of God.

CXVI. Also, that when the king of the Armenians, called Ethom, in order that the Armenians might unite with the Roman Church, had assembled all the bishops of Armenia, and the teachers and catholicons, that they might debate with the legate sent to them through the Roman Church, and that the said debate had taken place, the said king knew that the holy Roman Church held the truth, and that The Armenians were wandering from the truth, from that time the kings of Armenia Minor held the faith of the Holy Roman Church, but the bishops, teachers and princes of the Armenians were not satisfied with this. And after the departure of the said legate, a certain teacher, called Varta de Nigromonte, composed a book called De *Risma*, that is *Versus pede*, against the pope and his legate and against the Roman Church, in which he called the Roman pope a proud Pharaoh, with his subjects drowned in the sea of heresies and that his ambassador, Pharaoh's ambassador, had returned with the greatest shame; and he said that the Roman Church had been much deceived, because it had received birth and water from the accursed Arthomonus; and he wrote many other blasphemies in the said book, which is great. And many Armenian ministers and bishops and priests honor the said book as the canons of the Apostles.

CXVII. Also, that the Armenians do not have at all the true faith held by the Holy Roman Church nor the Sacraments, and they blaspheme the Holy Roman Church and the Pope and the Cardinals, saying that they are heretics; and what the Catholicon of Armenia Minor said, that the pope and all the cardinals every day kill men who have more hairs on their heads than he himself. And although they say that simony is not to be committed, yet they themselves do not give thanks without the corruption of simony; and there are very few people in Armenia Minor, besides the king and some nobles, who hold the faith of the Roman Church.

LATIN TEXT

CUM DUDUM (Aug. 1, 1341)

Libellus ad Armenios

In nomine Domini. Amen.

Cum dudum ad audientiam sanctissimi patris et domini nostri domini Benedicti divina providentia papae XII et etiam diu ante, dum erat in cardinalatus officio constitutus, ad audientiam felicis recordationis domini Joannis papae XXII praedecessoris sui saepissime pervenisset, quod Armeni in et de his quae ad fidem et credentiam pertinent christianam, communiter in utraque Armenia vel specialiter in una vel in alia Armenia aut aliquid de una vel de alia tenebant et docebant vel etiam praedicabant errores varios et diversos, tam contra divinam Scripturam, Concilia generalia, quam etiam contra illa quae determinavit, docet et docuit ac praedicavit et praedicat sancta Romana Ecclesia, mater omnium et magistra. Volens idem dominus noster papa super praedictis et eorum singulis inquirere ac scire plenius veritatem, ad sui praesentiam fecit venire plures Armenos et aliqui etiam ex eis venerunt ad eandem praesentiam per seipsos, aliquos etiam ex Latinis qui fuerant in partibus Armeniae audiverantque dictos Armenos errores multos dogmatizantes atque tenentes, fecit ad se venire, a quibus, Armenis et Latinis, videlicet ab aliquibus eorum, per dictum dominum nostrum papam et ab aliis per reverendum patrem dominum Bernardum tituli Sancti Cyriaci in Thermis presbyterum Cardinalem de mandato ipsius domini papae receptum extitit iuramentum, quod ipsi super praedictis et aliis quae in dictis partibus vel alibi ab eisdem Armenis audissent vel scirent ipsos tenere, docere vel praedicare, plenam et meram, tam de seipsis, ut de principalibus, quam de aliis personis, vivis et defunctis, ut testes confiterentur et deponerent veritatem. Ipsis itaque sic receptis et eis postmodum, videlicet illis qui linguam latinam nec loqui nec intelligere sciebant, per interpretes idoneos et aliis qui utramque linguam, scilicet armenam et latinam loqui et intelligere sciebant, per se necnon et quibusdam libris in armena lingua scriptis, ipsi domino nostro papae traditis per aliquos de dictis Armenis, quibus, ut plures ex eisdem Armenis asseruerunt et adhuc asserunt, communiter utuntur Armeni tam in Maiori Armenia quam Minori, diligenter examinatis, ad haec eis certo notario apostolico assignato, qui depositiones et confessiones dum fiebant et errores certos dum de praedictis libris interpretarentur seu extraherentur, per certas personas utramque linguam, sciscilicet armenam et latinam, intelligere ac loqui scientes, redigebat et redigit in scriptis. Consequenter ex depositionibus et confessionibus eorum inventum est dictos Armenos vel aliquos ex eis tenere, credere et docere articulos infrascriptos:

I. Et primo, quod aliqui antiqui magistri Armenorum dixerunt et praedicaverunt, quod Spiritus Sanctus procedit a Filio sicut et a Patre, sed a sexcentis et duodecim annis circa, magistri et praelati et alii Armeni de Maiori Armenia dimiserunt praedicare et dicere, quod Spiritus Sanctus procedat a Filio sicut et a Patre, quia dicto tempore factum fuit concilium apud Armenos, ubi fuerunt catholicon et episcopi ac magistri Armenorum et patriarcha Surianorum et ibi determinaverunt, quod de cetero non diceretur apud eos, quod Spiritus Sanctus procederet a Filio sicut et a Patre; et condemnaverunt antiquos doctores Armenorum, qui fuerunt ante dictum concilium, eo quod dixerant et docuerant quod Spiritus Sanctus procedit a Filio sicut et a Patre; et extunc omnes Armenos, qui tenuerunt et docuerunt quod Spiritus Sanctus procedebat a Filio, sicut et a Patre, persecuti sunt, incarcerando eos et in vinculis ponendo. Et sic apud Armenos nullus audet hoc dicere vel docere, nisi soli illi <qui> reuniti sunt sanctae Romanae Ecclesiae. Et si quandoque inveniatur in libris eorum positum, quod Spiritus Sanctus procedat a Filio, hanc processionem <de> temporali, ad santificandam creaturam et non de processione eius aeterna, qua processit aeternaliter a Patre et Filio in esse personaliter intelligendam dicunt.

II. Item, quod Armeni articulum fidei in Symbolo positum de Spiritu Sancto, sic pronuntiant: Credo in Spiritum Sanctum increatum et perfectum, qui locutus est in Lege et Prophetis et Evangeliis et descendit in Iordane et praedicavit in Apostolis et habitat in Sanctis — nullam mentionem facientes, quod Spiritus Sanctus procedat a Patre vel a Patre et Filio. — Quando tamen legunt evangelium Joannis, ubi dicitur quod Paraclitus procedit a Patre, hoc dicunt et confitentur; sed multi ex eis negant quod Spiritus Sanctus procedat a Filio; et si aliqui hoc credant, tamen non audent hoc manifeste dicere. Et licet in concilio Chalcedonensi non fuerit determinatum expresse, quod Spiritus Sanctus procederet a Filio sicut a Patre, sed hoc fuerat determinatum in conciliis Constantinopolitano et Ephesino quia tamen concilium

Chalcedonense approbavit determinata in dictis conciliis prioribus, ideo, reprobando dictum concilium Chalcedonense, dicti Armeni reprobarunt dicta concilia quae per dictum concilium approbata fuerunt, inter quae erat, quod Spiritus Sanctus procedit a Filio sicut et a Patre.

III. Item, quod in dicto concilio reprobaverunt concilium Chalcedonense ex eo principaliter, quod in dicto concilio Chalcedonensi fuerat determinatum, quod in domino Iesu Christo erant duae naturae, humana scilicet et divina, et unica persona subsistens in duabus naturis; et in dicto concilio determinaverunt, quod sicut in domino Iesu Christo erat unica persona, ita erat una natura, scilicet divina, et una voluntas et una operatio, et anathematizaverunt dicentes contrarium; et illos qui contrarium dicebant perscuti sunt, eos incarcerando, vinculando et morti tradendo. In dicto etiam concilio damnaverant *beatum Leonem* papam et epistolas eius quas miserat ad concilium Chalcedonense et ad Flavianum patriarcham Constantinopolitanum, in quibus beatus Leo scripserat, quod in domino Iesu Christo erant duae naturae et una persona, duae voluntates et duae operaciones. In dicto etiam concilio Dioscorum condemnatum per dictum concilium Chalcedonense canonizaverunt et pro Sancto haberi voluerunt et adhuc ter in anno faciunt festum de eo sicut de Sancto et eum laudant ut Sanctum; et maledicunt beatum Leonem et concilium Chalcedonense, qui damnaveverunt dictum Dioscorum. Dicunt etiam quod illi qui consenserunt determinatis in dicto concilio Chalcedonensi, Christum negaverunt.

IV. Item, quod Armeni dicunt et tenent, quod peccatum primorum parentum personale ipsorum tam grave fuit, quod omnes eorum filii ex semine eorum propagati, usque ad Christi passionem, merito dicti peccati personalis ipsorum damnati fuerunt et in inferno post mortem detrusi, non propter hoc quod ipsi ex Adam aliquod peccatum originale contraxerint, cum dicant pueros nullum omnino habere originale peccatum nec ante Christi passionem nec post; sed dicta damnatio ante Christi passionem eos sequebatur ratione gravitatis peccati personalis, quod commiserunt Adam et Eva transgrediendo divinum praeceptum eis datum, sed post Domini passionem, in qua peccatum primorum parentum deletum fuit, pueri qui nascuntur ex filiis Adam non sunt damnationi addicti nec in inferno ratione dicti peccati sunt detrudendi, quia Christus totaliter peccatum primorum parentum delevit in sua passione.

V. Item, quod quidam magister Armenorum vocatus Mechitariz, qui interpretatur Paraclitus, de novo introduxit et docuit, quod anima humana filii propagatur ab anima patris sui, sicut corpus a corpore et angelus etiam unus ab alio; quia, cum anima humana rationalis existens et angelus existens intellectualis naturae sint quaedam lumina spiritualia, ex se ipsis propagant alia lumina spiritualia; et in hoc sequuntur eum quasi omnes de provincia Argiciensi, quae est magna provincia, continens septem dietas. Alii vero Armeni non dicunt hoc, sed quod Deus omnes animas creat. Et Armeni de dicta provincia habent illum Mechitariz pro Sancto.

VI. Item dicunt Armeni, quod animae puerorum qui nascuntur ex christianis parentibus post Christi passionem, si moriantur antequam baptizentur, vadunt ad paradisum terrestrem, in quo fuit Adam ante peccatum; animae vero puerorum qui nascuntur ex parentibus non christianis post Christi passionem et moriuntur sine baptismo, vadunt ad loca ubi sunt animae parentum ipsorum.

VII. Item, quod dicti Armeni dicunt, quod animae hominum adultorum, qui mortui sunt vel morientur post Christi passionem, vadunt in aere vel in terra, quae est iuxta paradisum terrestrem, vel alibi, ubi Deus ordinat ipsas manere usque ad diem Iudicii, sive sint christiani sive non; nulla tamen animae ipsorum vadit ad infernum vel paradisum caelestem vel terrestrem, usque ad dictum tempus Iudicii. Et, ut dicunt, animae puerorum non baptizatorum ad Generale Iudicium venient cum corporibus suis et post iudicium ibunt ad paradisum terrestrem, in quo volabunt sicut columbae de una arbore ad aliam et sicut angeli de coelo ad terram et de una parte terrae ad aliam; non tamen habebunt gloriam nec sustinebunt poenam aliquam. Post generale iudicium animae adultorum ibunt ad loca quae eis deputabuntur post dictum Generale Iudicium.

VIII. Item, quod Armeni dicunt, quod animae puerorum baptizatorum et animae multum perfectorum hominum post Generale Iudicium intrabunt in regnum caelorum, ubi carebunt omni malo poenali huius vitae, quia nec esurient nec sitient nec alios defectus humani corporis sentient, nec nubent nec nubentur, sedebunt sicuti angeli Dei in caelis, neo peccare poterunt nec cadere a statu in quo erant. Non tamen videbunt Dei essentiam, quia nulla creatura eam videre potest; sed videbunt claritatem Dei, quae ab eius essentia manat, sicut lux solis emanat a sole et tamen non est sol; et in dicta visione dictae claritatis erunt diversi gradus, ita quod perfectius dictam claritatem videbunt angeli quam quicumque bomines, et prophetae et Apostoli ac martyres et virgines, quam pueri baptizati; et in hoc dicunt, quod consistet Sanctorum perfectorum et puerorum baptizatorum beatitudo.

IX. Item, de pueris non baptizatis et de non perfecte iustis hominibus, qui scilicet non pervenerunt ad perfectionem Apostolorum, martyrum, confessorum et virginum, Armeni dicunt, quod post Generale Iudicium ibunt ad paradisum terrestrem et non coelestem, ubi carebunt omni molestia corporali et delectabuntur inter ligna paradisi; non tamen comedent nec bibent nec nubent nec nubentur, et ita perpetuo ibi manebunt, et in hoc consistet eorum beatitudo. Differentia tamen erit inter pueros non baptizatos christianorum, filios et adultos non perfecte iustos; quia adulti non perfecte iusti habebunt coronam de lumine ignis quo terra comburetur ante Iudicium; videbunt etiam claritatem ligni Crucis Christi, quae claritas tunc maxima erit; quia omnes claritates quae sunt in hoc mundo, adiungentur claritati Crucis Christi et dicti adulti secundum quod magis vel minus perfecti erunt, dictas coronas luminis differentes habebunt et dictam claritatem Crucis Christi differenter videbunt, secundum eorum merita; dictas tamen coronas luminis non habebunt pueri non baptizati nec videbunt claritatem Crucis Christi; et in hoc erit differentia inter eos.

X. Item dicunt, quod mediocriter homines mali christiani, post Generale Iudicium non ibunt ad paradisum caelestem vel terrestrem, sed manebunt in terra, in qua nunc habitant homines, quae tota erit plena arboribus, sicut paradisus terrestris, et tamen non comedent nec bibunt nec ex tunc morientur; et hic locus dabitur eis ex hoc, quod mediocriter mali fuerunt. Vocant autem homines mediocriter malos, homines coniugatos et alios in saeculo communiter viventes.

XI. Item, de multum malis hominibus, sicut sunt generaliter omnes infideles et christiani malam vitam et peccatricem ducentes, habent duas opiniones, quarum una est, quod tales post Generale Iudicium ponentur in Oceanum, quod tunc erit igneum et ibi graviter cruciabuntur per vermes qui ibi erunt, qui ita magni erunt sicut dracones; et sicut magis vel minus peccaverunt, ita dicti dracones vel maiores vel minores erunt; quia, ut dicunt, statim quando homo graviter peccat, dictus draco nascitur in Oceano et crescit secundum quod plus vel minus homo peccat; et aliqui ex hominibus malis, qui multa peccata et diversa commiserunt, plures dracones ibi habebunt, quorum unus cruciabit eos in oculis et alter in auribus et sic de aliis membris. Cruciabuntur etiam ibi daemones, qui ibi cum eis erunt, iuxta illud quod Dominus dicturus est malis: *Ite in ignem aeternum, qui paratus est diabolo et angelis eius*; et ita perpetuo ibi mali homines cruciabuntur. — Alia vero eorum opinio dicit, quae magis communis est apud Armenos, quod post generale iudicium nullus Infernus erit, nec mine est, nec fuit postquam Christus ad inferos descendit et Infernum totaliter destruxit, sed unusquisque peccator <a> peccato quod commisit cruciabitur et secundum quod plus vel minus peccavit, secundum hoc plus vel minus a dictis peccatis cruciabitur; et sic talia peccata dicuntur esse Infernus, in quo peccatores post Generale Iudicium cruciabuntur.

XII. Item, praedicti Armeni dicunt, quod homines mediocriter mali in Iudicio cum operibus suis ponentur in statera et si plus ponderaverint eorum mala quam bona, tunc ponentur in Oceanum, secundum praedictam opinionem de qua supra dictum est et affligentur ibi secundum quod demeruerunt. Si vero plus ponderaverint eorum bona quam mala, tunc ponentur in ista terra, quae erit arboribus plena, non tamen ita delectabilis sicut est paradisus terrestris. Si vero bona eorum et mala aequaliter ponderent, tunc ad preces beatae Mariae et aliorum Sanctorum Deus ponet eos in ista terra, in qua nullum malum afflictivum patientur.

XIII. Item, licet in Ordinario Armenorum contineatur, quod illi qui baptizantur, etiamsi pueri sint, qui veniunt ad baptismum de diaboli servitute, tamen dicunt, quod tales pueri nullum peccatum habent, sed sicut omnino innocentes et omni peccato, etiam originali, immunes; nec dicunt quod baptizentur, ut consequantur remissionem peccatorum, sed ut sint christiani et ut post Generale Iudicium intrent cum perfectis Sanctis in regnum caelorum; et ad haec duo valet eis baptismus secundum eos.

XIV. Item, quod dicti Armeni dicunt et tenent, quod Christus descendens ad inferos praedicavit ibi et illas animas quae ei credere voluerunt, iustificavit, illas autem quae ei credere noluerunt, in suo peccato dereliquit. Exiens autem ab inferis, destruxit totaliter infernum et omnes animas quas ibi invenit, sive essent bonae sive essent malae, inde eduxit et posuit eas in isto aere et terra et circa paradisum terrestrem, ubi erunt usque ad finale iudicium. Interim tamen animae mediocriter malae et malae simpliciter, non patientur aliquam poenam sensibilem, sed solum patiuntur timorem; mediocriter quidem malae, quia timent suum periculum, quod erit in die iudicii, ut supra scriptum est, quando ponentur in statera; malae vero simpliciter, quia timent poenam Oceani, ubi ponentur post Generale Iudicium, patiuntur poenam timoris, quae eas multum affligit mentaliter. Mediocriter vero bonas et perfecte bonas posuit in ista terra vel aere circa paradisum terrestrem; et, ut dicunt, tales animae sunt in magna consolatione propter spem quam habent de remuneratione quam consecuturae sunt post Generale Iudicium. Et dicunt, quod ante dictum Generale Iudicium non erit remuneratio alia operum bonorum vel malorum, inducentes ad hoc dictum Apostoli: *Oportet nos praesentari ante tribunal Christi, ut recipiat unus quisque prout in corpore gessit, sive bonum fuerit sive malum.*

XV. Item, quod dicti Armeni non dicunt nec tenent, quod Christus descendens ad inferos praedicaverit daemonibus nec quod daemones eduxerit de Inferno, sed bene dicunt quod daemones usque ad Generale Iudicium sunt in isto aere vel in terra. Si tamen ibi existentes aliquam poenam sensibilem sustinent vel sustinebunt usque ad dictum Generale Iudicium, non exprimunt; dicunt tamen quod patiuntur carentiam gloriae et quod ipsi, qui prius erant clari, effecti sunt nigri; et quod multum timent poenam Oceani, in qua ponendi sunt post Generale Iudicium cum malis hominibus.

XVI. Item, quod inter Armenos sunt duae opiniones de tempore quo creati fuerunt angeli; quia aliqui eorum dicunt, quod ante istum mundum sensibilem angeli creati fuerunt; alii vero dicunt, quod cum isto mundo sensibili creati fuerunt, scilicet cum caelo empireo, ante omnem diem. Dicunt etiam, quod omnes angeli boni creati fuerunt et in dicta bonitate steterunt, ut eorum aliqui dicunt, usque ad quartam diem, quando Deus luminaria fecit; aliqui vero eorum dicunt quod sexta die, quando Adam creatus fuit, daemones peccaverunt et de caelo ceciderunt per illam partem caeli quae apud eos dicitur

Arocea, apud nos vero dicitur Galaxia; cum quibus etiam per dictum foramen unus bonus angelus cecidit et multi alii cecidissent, nisi Deus eis dixisset: *Pax vobis,* ille vero bonus angelus qui ceciderat, ad preces beati Basilii restitutus in caelo fuit. Dicunt etiam eorum aliqui, quod feria sexta de inane Adam creatus fuit, sed circa sextam dictae diei Eva fuit formata et secundum aliquos eorum eadem die fuit per diabolum tentata, secundum vero alios feria sexta sequentis septimanae. Dicunt etiam, quod nullus bonorum angelorum unquam efficietur malus, nec malus bonus.

XVII. Item, quod Armeni communiter tenent, quod in alio saeculo non est purgatorium animarum, quia, ut dicunt, si christianus confiteatur peccata sua, omnia peccata eius et poenae peccatorum ei dimittuntur. Nec etiam ipsi orant pro defunctis, ut eis in alio saeculo peccata dimittantur, sed generaliter orant pro omnibus mortuis, sicut pro b. Maria, Apostolis, martyribus et aliis Sanctis, ut in die iudicii intrent in regnum caeleste vel in aliis locis, ut supra dictum est, et quod ibi requiescant. De animabus vero paganorum dicunt, quod animae eorum sunt super sepulchra ipsorum vel in sepulchris, usque ad diem iudicii et frequenter audiuntur in sepulchris Saracenorum voces et mugitus et etiam quandoque animae eorum vel daemones pro eis videntur circa sepulchra ipsorum in diversis speciebus animalium vel hominum; propter quod Saraceni non libenter stant circa sepulchra Saracenorum et ex hoc etiam quandoque Saraceni faciunt baptizari suos filios et inungi in diversis locis, ut post mortem non egrediantur de sepulchris; non tamen faciunt eos baptizari, ut efficiantur christiani.

XVIII. Item, quod Armeni credunt et tenent, quod Christus descendit de caelo et incarnatus fuit propter hominum salutem, non pro eo, quod filii propagati ex Adam et Eva post peccatum eorum ex eis contrahant originale peccatum, a quo per Christi incarnationem et mortem salventur, cum nullum tale peccatum dicant esse in filiis Adae, sed dicunt quod Christus propter salutem hominum est incarnatus et passus, quia per suam passionem filii Adam, qui dictam passionem praecesserunt, fuerunt liberati ab Inferno in quo erant non ratione originalis peccati, quod in eis esset, sed ratione gravitatis peccati personalis primorum parentum. Credunt etiam, quod Christus propter salutem puerorum, qui nati fuerunt post eius passionem, incarnatus fuit et passus, quia per suam passionem destruxit totaliter Infernum, et ita post eius passionem nullus ex dictis pueris vadit ad Infernum. Credunt etiam, quod propter salutem hominum adultorum christianorum Christus fuerit incarnatus et passus, quia si tales poeniteant de peccatis suis post eius passionem, quando moriuntur non vadunt ad infernum.

XIX. Item, quod Armeni credunt et tenent, quod primi parentes et tota eorum posteritas usque ad Christi passionem mortua fuit in corpore et in anima ad Infernum descendit non propter originale peccatum, quod filii Adam contraxerunt ab Adam, sed ratione gravitatis peccati personalis primorum parentum; propter quod, licet eorum filii non peccaverint, tamen propter peccatum primorum parentum passi fuerunt et mortem corporalem et apud inferos punitae eorum animae fuerunt usque ad dictum tempus. Credunt etiam et tenent, quod post Christi passionem et ante, usque ad generalem resurrectionem filii Adam habent concupiscentiam inordinatam carnis et mortalitatem propter gravitatem peccati primorum parentum et non propter originale peccatum quod ex eis contraxerint; a qua concupiscentia et mortalitate Sancti liberabuntur in generali resurrectione per Christum; et in tantum dicunt, quod dicta concupiscentia carnis est peccatum et malum, quod parentes etiam christiani quando matrimonialiter concubunt committunt peccatum; et propter hoc poenitentia eis imponitur per sacerdotes, quia actum matrimonialem dicunt esse peccatum et etiam matrimonium. Credunt etiam et tenent, quod si Adam et Eva non fuissent transgressi Dei mandatum, non fuisset inter eos carnalis commixtio nec per seminum commixtionem fieret generatio humana, sed homines propagarentur ab hominibus sine carnali commixtione, sicut lumen propagatur a lumine. Dicunt etiam, quod Deus, praesciens quod homines transgredirentur eius praeceptum, membra genitalia fecit in eis, per quae post peccatum fieret hominum propagatio.

XX. Item, quod Armeni credunt et tenent, quod aeternus Dei Filius natus de substantia Patris, in tempore sibi univit humanam naturam et factus fuit homo, sic tamen, quod in ipsa unione humanae naturae ad Dei Filium, humana natura conversa fuit in divinam eius naturam, sic quod post dictam unionem in Christo non est nisi una natura, scilicet divina et non humana, sicut ipse est una persona. Et dicti Armeni maledicunt omnes illos qui contrarium dicunt et in tantum detestantur illos qui dicunt post unionem duas naturas esse in Christo, divinam scilicet et humanam; quod si aliquis Armenus, prius baptizatus secundum ritum eorum, hoc diceret, non communicant cum eo, sed habent eum ac si paganus fuisset; et si vult reverti ad fidem Armenorum, eum rebaptizant, sic <acsi> semper paganus fuisset, et post secundum baptismum imponunt ei poenitentiam viginti annorum.

XXI. Item, quod Armeni credunt et tenent, quod quia secundum eos, post unionem naturarum in Christo, natura humana conversa fuit in naturam divinam, ita quod in Christo ex tunc non fuit nisi natura divina, cum dicta natura divina in Christo fuit passibilis et impassibilis, mortalis et immortalis, secundum quod Christo placebat, sic dicunt Christum fuisse passum et mortuum secundum naturam divinam, quia sic voluit ipse, licet humana natura in eo non esset, quando passus et mortuus fuit. Credunt etiam et tenent, quod in domino Iesu Christo post unionem non fuit nisi unus intellectus, una voluntas et una operatio, scilicet divina et non humana.

XXII. Item, quod Armeni dicunt et tenent, quod ab illa hora, qua Dominus mortuus fuit in cruce, ipse descendit ad inferos et Infernum destruxit totaliter; ita quod ex tunc non fuit Infernus nec aliquae animae hominum vel etiam daemones ex tunc fuerunt in Inferno nec erunt postea; quando vero Christus resurrexit, educens de Inferno Sanctorum animas quae ibidem erant, duxit eas in paradisum terrestrem et cum ipsis dictum paradisum intravit, dicens eis: *Ecce locus in quo fuistis;* et statim de dicto paradiso eas eiecit et posuit eas in terra vel aëre circa paradisum terrestrem.

XXIII. Item, quod de anima latronis Christum confitentis in cruce, apud Armenos sunt diversae opiniones: quarum una est, quod illud quod ponitur in Evangelio: *Hodie mecum eris in paradiso; hodie,* non tenetur ibi determinate pro illa die qua mortui fuerunt Dominus et latro, sed tenetur pro die finalis iudicii, quando Sancti perfecti intrabunt in paradisum caelestem, quomodo dies accipitur in psalmo: *Melior est dies una in atriis tuis*; tunc enim, et non ante, latro intrabit in paradisum caelestem, secundum eos, cum aliis Sanctis perfectis. Alia vero opinio eorum dicit, quod die qua dictus latro mortuus fuit, eius anima venit ad portam paradisi terrestris volens illuc intrare; sed per Angelos et Enoch et Eliam intrare illuc prohibitus fuit; sed in die resurrectionis Domini, quando Dominus cum aliis animabus Sanctorum, quas extraxerat de

Inferno, venit ad portam paradisi terrestris, invenit ibi dictam animam latronis, et cum Dominus ostendisset manus et latus Angelis et Enoch et Eliae, aperientes ei portam paradisi, intravit illuc cum dicta anima latronis et aliorum Sanctorum et cum eis dixisset: *Ecce locus de quo exivistis;* cum omnibus dictis animabus exivit de paradiso et eas posuit in terra vel in aere circa dictum paradisum, ubi erunt usque ad diem Iudicii; et tunc introducentur in paradisum coelestem. Alii vero dicunt, quod illa hora, qua Adam exivit de paradiso feria sexta, Dominus posuit animam latronis in paradiso terrestri; si tamen postea inde eduxit eam vel non, non dicunt.

XXIV. Item, quod dicti Armeni dicunt et tenent, quod animae malorum hominum, quae multa peccata actualia gravia commiserunt, qui mortui fuerunt ante Christi Passionem, fuerunt positae in Inferno, et ibi poenas infernales pro peccatis suis sustinuerunt; sed cum Dominus post suam Passionem Infernum destruxisset, dictas animas posuit in terra vel in aere; et ibi vadunt huc et illuc, non patientes aliquam poenam sensibilem, usque ad diem Iudicii. Hominum autem malignorum animae, qui fuerunt post Domini Passionem, quando mortui sunt dicti homines, angeli mali et terribiles accipiunt eas et adducunt ad Oceanum, de quo supra mentio facta est, et ostendunt eis Oceanum et vermes vel dracones, qui ibi sunt; et dicunt eis, quod post Generale Iudicium ibi ponentur et per dictum Oceanum et dracones cruciabuntur; et ex hoc dictae animae multum timent propter dictas poenas, quas passurae sunt post Generale Iudicium; non tamen interim aliam poenam sensibilem patientur. Animae vero hominum bonorum et perfectorum, quando mortui sunt, accipiuntur per bonos angelos et ducuntur in caelum ante thronum Dei; et vident sub throno Dei, qui thronus sunt angeli, gloriam quam post generale iudicium habiturae sunt; et de hoc multum consolantur; postea tamen ab angelis ducuntur ad terram vel ad aërem et sunt ibi usque ad diem Iudicii et propter dictam spem requiescere dicuntur. Dicunt etiam et credunt, quod post Generale Iudicium homines mali, qui fuerunt vel ante Domini Passionem vel post, ponentur in corpore et in anima in dicto Oceano et ibi cruciabuntur perpetuo.

XXV. Item, quod Armeni dicentes unam solam naturam esse in Christo, scilicet divinam et non humanam, respondere non possunt ad dicta posita in Scriptura, per quae manifeste ostenditur Christum habuisse humanam animam, quae divina natura non erat, sicut: *Non derelinquere animam meam in inferno*; nec ad illud: *Tristis est amima mea usque ad mortem*; nec ad illud, quod dicit Petrus, quod spiritualiter descendens, praedicavit in Inferno; nec ad illud, quod Dominus dicit: *Pater in manus tuas commendo spiritum meum et inclinato capite emisit spiritum*. Per quae omnia manifeste Scriptura dicit, fuisse in Christo post unionem animam humanam. Sed cum eis praedicta dicuntur, non habentes quid respondeant, recurrunt ad baculos vel ad poenas corporales, ut male tractent illos, qui talia eis dicunt. Dicunt etiam et credunt, quod anima Christi quando descendit ad inferos, ne cognosceretur, induit se deitate, sicut et quando erat in vita praesenti, ne cognosceretur, induit deitatem suam corpore.

XXVI. Item, quod Armeni dicunt et credunt, quod licet resurrectio a morte solum ad carnem pertineat, quae mortua fuerat, tamen in Christo, quia non erat nisi divina natura post unionem, ipsa secundum quod volebat faciebat opera carnis et opera animae, quamvis in Christo nec caro esset nec anima post unionem.

XXVII. Item, quod Armeni credunt et tenent, quod die sabbati post Parasceven hora sexta Dominus resurrexit; et hoc dicunt se habere ex traditione Gregorii, qui fuit antiquus eorum catholicon, cui, ut dicunt, fuit revelatum, cum esset in Sepulchro Domini, quod hora sexta dictae diei sabbati resurrexerat Dominus; et sic apud Armenos est determinatum; et dicta hora faciunt festum de resurrectione Domini; et postea eadem die comedunt ova et caseum, non tamen carnes. Computant autem tres dies et noctes, quibus fuit Dominus in ventre terrae sic, quia in nocte sequente feriam quintam Dominus tradidit corpus suum et sanguinem discipulis suis, qui terrei erant, corpus eius et sanguinem comederunt et biberunt et sic in seipsis Christum sepeliverunt; et computant illam noctem; et postea diem sequentem usque ad illam horam, qua in die Parasceves tenebrae factae sunt super universam terram, pro prima die et nocte; tempus vero illud, quo dictae tenebrae duraverunt, computant pro secunda nocte; et diem, qui fuit post dictas tenebras, computant pro secunda die; noctem quae praecedit sabbatum, computant pro tertia nocte; et diem sabbati usque ad meridiem pro tertia die; et dicunt quod praedicta eorum opinio confirmata fuit per beatum Silvestrum papam ad instantiam dicti Gregorii; et plus credunt dictae opinioni quam evangeliis Marci et Lucae, qui dicunt, quod prima sabbati, id est dominica, Dominus resurrexit.

XXVIII. Item, quod Armeni nesciunt respondere ad illa, quae in Evangeliis continentur, ubi manifeste scribitur, quod Christus post suam resurrectionem verum corpus humanum habuit, cum dicant, quod in ipsa unione humana natura conversa fuit in deitatem; nisi hoc solum, quod voluntas divina secundum quod volebat faciebat et ostendebat se corpus humanum habere, cum tamen non haberet.

XXIX. Item, licet secundum Armenos in Christo post unionem non fuerit nisi natura divina, in quam conversa fuit humana eius natura, Armeni tamen dicunt et tenent, quod voluntati Christi subiecta erat divina natura, ut de ea faceret quod vellet; et ita, ut dicunt, quando voluit divina eius natura, mortalis fuit et etiam mortua, et quando voluit facta fuit immortalis, sicut factum fuit post suam resurrectionem, accipientes ad hoc probandum illud quod dicitur in Joanne: *Ego vivo, et vos vivetis.*

XXX. Item, Armeni dicunt et tenent, quod ex hoc quod Christus ascendit in caelum, in eo post unionem desiit esse humana natura; alioquin si in ipso fuisset humana natura post unionem, non ascendisset in caelum, sed translatus fuisset in paradisum terrestrem, sicut factum fuit de Elia et Enoch.

XXXI. Item, quod Armeni tenent, quod illae auctoritates Prophetae et Apostoli: *Ascendens Christus in altum, captivam duxit captivitatem,* et quod Christus expoliavit Principatus et Potestates et transduxit eas in semetipsum, non intelliguntur, quod hoc fecerit quando Christus ascendit in caelum, sed intelligunt quando Christus, ascendens ab inferis, eduxit secum animas hominum quae ibi erant et posuit eas in ista terra vel aere usque ad diem iudicii.

XXXII. Item, quod Armeni dicunt et tenent, quod Christus ascendens ad inferos, ligavit daemones qui ibi erant et etiam super terram, ut non possent tentare vel offendere homines sicut ante faciebant; sed sunt iam trecenti anni, quod omnes daemones sunt disligati et seduxerunt homines a fide Christi per totum mundum, exceptis Armenis; sed a triginta annis citra illos homines de Minori Armenia et a viginti quinque annis citra Armenos de Maiori Armenia seduxerunt a fide Christi, quia, ut dicunt, ex tunc Armeni posuerunt in

Sacrificio aquam in vino et fecerunt festum Nativitatis Domini vigesima quinta die decembris et sic, a daemonibus seducti, fidem Christi dimiserunt.

XXXIII. Item, quod Armeni dicunt et tenent, quod Christus post suam ascensionem habuit humanitatem, sed non habuit naturam humanam, nec voluntatem nec operationem humanam. Dicunt etiam et tenent, quod Christus in caelum ascendens non subito pervenit ad dexteram Patris, sed in decima die post suam ascensionem et in novem diebus qui sunt a die ascensionis eius usque ad diem Pentecostes, Christus fuit inter angelos, ita quod per unum diem fuit in uno ordine angelorum et alio die in alio et quilibet ordo angelorum festivavit eum una die; decima vero die pervenit ad dexteram Patris et tunc statim misit Apostolis Spiritum Sanctum et propter hoc Armeni festivant illas decem dies.

XXXIV. Item, quod Armeni de Maiori Armenia dicunt et tenent, quod ipsi sunt Ecclesia catholica et apostolica et propter hoc ipsi habent Catholicon et etiam eorum Ecclesia est apostolice, quia ipsi tenent fidein quam Apostoli praedicaverunt; et propter hoc sunt Ecclesia catholica et apostolica. Graeca vero ecclesia non est Ecclesia catholica vel apostolica, quia ponunt aquam in vino in Sacrificio et quia dicunt duas naturas esse in Christo et quia faciunt festum Nativitatis Domini vigesima quinta die mensis decembris. Dicunt etiam et tenent, quod Ecclesia Romana non est Ecclesia catholica et apostolica, propter easdem causas quas dicunt de ecclesia graeca et etiam quia corrupit fidem christianam, faciendo et acceptando concilium Chalcedonense ad instantiam beati Leonis papae. Dicunt etiam et tenent, quod Ecclesia Romana et Graeca esse desinent ante generalem resurrectionem vel tempore Antichristi; ecclesia vero Armenorum durabit usque ad finem; et quod illi de Armenia Minori, exceptis rege et quibusdam nobilibus, sunt de Ecclesia Maioris Armeniae et sunt peiores quam illi de Maiore Armenia, nec volunt recipere aliquem magistrum, nisi sit de Maiori Armenia. Dicunt etiam quod rex et nobiles Minoris Armeniae, quia tenent supradictos articulos cum Ecclesia Romana et Graeca, non sunt de Ecclesia catholica et apostolica.

XXXV. Item, Armeni dicunt et tenent, quod Ecclesia Catholica fuit per totum orbem diffusa a principio, quia aliqui ex omnibus gentibus crediderunt in Christum; sed postea in concilio Chalcedonensi fuit fides Ecclesiae corrupta et destructa, ex eo, quod ibi determinatum fuit, quod in Christo erant duae naturae et una persona; et omnes qui dictum concilium receperunt, fuerunt... (sic!) Ecclesiam Catholicam; et quia dicti Armeni dictum concilium non receperunt, sed condemnaverunt, ideo solum apud eos est Ecclesia Catholica, exceptis paucis de ecclesia Minoris Armeniae.

XXXVI. Item, quod Armeni credunt et tenent, quod solum apud ipsos est una Ecclesia Catholica, quia, ut dicunt, apud eos sunt illa quae faciunt esse unam sanctam Ecclesiam, scilicet unus baptismus et unica fides Christi et unus Spiritus Sanctus et unus Deus et dominus; quae apud alias Ecclesias quae vocantur christianae, non sunt, quia, ut dicunt, Armeni habent verum baptismum, propter quod omnes venientes ad se de aliis Ecclesiis rebaptizant, immo, ut dicunt, verius baptizant, quia baptismum datum in aliis Ecclesiis non reputant esse verum baptismum. Habent etiam, ut dicunt, veram fidem, quam aliae Ecclesiae destruxerunt recipiendo concilium Chalcedonense. Habent etiam verum Spiritum Sanctum et verum Deum et dominum, quae aliae Ecclesiae non habent, quia negaverunt Deum et dominum in concilio Chalcedonensi, dicendo quod in Christo sunt duae naturae et una persona; propter quae in symbolo non dicunt simpliciter: *Et in unam sanctam ecclesiam;* sed *in istam sanctam ecclesiam*; accipiendo ly *istam*, pro ecclesia Armenorum.

XXXVII. Item, quod a tempore Heraclii imperatoris citra, fuerunt tres catholicon in Armenia, tenentes diversam fidem et diversum baptismum ab invicem; nam catholicon Columbarum dicit, quod Pater et Filius et Spiritus Sanctus fuerunt crucifixi in cruce; et illi qui sunt subiecti ei, baptizant in aqua; catholicon vero medius et subiecti eius dicunt, quod solus Dei Filius fuit crucifixus in cruce; et pro maiori parte baptizant in aqua, pauci tamen baptizant in vino, non tamen baptizatos mergunt *In nomine Patris, et Filii et Spiritus Sancti;* catholicon vero tertius a quinquaginta annis citra tenet illud, quod tenet ecclesia Graecorum. Conveniunt tamen dicti tres catholicon et subiecti eorum in istis, quod in Christo est una natura, sicut una persona, quae natura est divina; et quod non ponunt aquam in vino in Sacrificio, nec faciunt festum Nativitatis Domini vigesima quinta die decembris, excepto catholicon tertio, qui a quinquaginta annis citra in istis a primis duobus est separatus; quilibet autem de dictis catholicon dicit, quod ipse tenet veram fidem et verum baptismum habet et quod alii catholicon ab eo non habent veram fidem nec verum baptisma; et sic quia sunt diversi inter se, non est una Ecclesia inter eos, sed alia et alia.

XXXVIII. Item, quod Armeni credunt et tenent, quod in aliis Ecclesiis ab Ecclesiis Armenorum non datur peccatorum remissio, quia aliae ecclesiae negaverunt veram fidem, recipiendo concilium Chalcedonense; nec etiam habent verum baptismum, quia miscent aquam in vino in sacrificio, dicentes quod aqua quae fluxit de latere Christi virtutem tribuit soli sacramento baptismi; et ideo illae Ecclesiae, quae miscent aquam in vino, baptismum perdiderunt; propter quod peccatorum remissio non fit apud ipsos, sed solum fit in ecclesia Armenorum; et ideo presbyteri Armenorum prohibent subiectis suis, ne Sacramenta recipiant ab aliis, quam ab Armenis, quia illa Sacramenta alii non habent.

XXXIX. Item, quod Armeni dicunt et tenent, quod populus subiectus uni catholicon potest recipere dicta sacramenta ab alio catholicon vel presbyteris eius et dicta sacramenta valent dicto populo; sed episcopi et presbyteri unius catholicon non possunt recipere sacramenta ab alio catholicon vel subiectis eius et si reciperent talia sacramenta, eis non valerent.

XL. Item, Armeni credunt et tenent, quod nullus Armenus potest consequi remissionem peccatorum per episcopos vel presbyteros Ecclesiae Romanae vel Graecae; sed aliqui ex Armenis dicunt, quod peccatorum remissio potest fieri in Armenis per episcopos et presbyteros Armenorum; alii vero dicunt quod episcopi vel presbyteri Armenorum nihil faciunt ad peccatorum remissionem nec principaliter nec ministerialiter, sed solus Deus peccata remittit; nec episcopi vel presbyteri adhibentur ad faciendam dictam peccatorum remissionem, nisi quia ipsi acceperunt potestatem loquendi a Deo; et ideo cum absolvunt dicunt: *Deus dimittat tibi peccata tua* vel: *Ego dimitto tibi peccata tua in terra et Deus dimittat tibi in caelis.*

XLI. Item, Armeni dicunt et tenent, quod postquam aliquis peccando perdidit gratiam Dei, numquam postea in aequali gratia resurgit.

XLII. Item, Armeni dicunt et tenent, quod sola Christi passio, sine omni alio Dei dono, etiam gratificante, sufficit ad peccatorum remissionem; nec dicunt, quod ad peccatorum remissionem faciendam requiratur gratia Dei gratificans vel iustificans nec quod in Sacramentis Novae Legis detur gratia gratificans.

XLIII. Item, Armeni dicunt et tenent, quod liberum arbitrium humanum non sufficit sibi ad peccandum, sed diabolus facit et instigat homines ad peccandum; ita quod si daemones non essent, nullus homo peccaret.

XLIV. Item, licet Armeni orent in Missa et alias pro bonis tam spiritualibus quam temporalibus adipiscendis et pro malis removendis, pro mortuis tamen non orant, ut in praesenti requiem obtineant, sed tantummodo in futuro.

XLV. Item, quod apud Armenos, quando aliquis ex eis mortuus est, talis observatio fit: quod de sero ducuntur animalia munda secundum Legem Moysi, cuiusmodi sunt oves, caprae et boves, coopertae pannis sericis ad ostium ecclesiae; ad quem locum exeunt clerici dictae ecclesiae et sacerdos benedicit sal et de sale benedicto ponit in ore dictorum animalium; et postea cum oleo de lino inunguntur dicta animalia; et deinde, effuso ipsorum sanguine, occiduntur et de carnibus dictorum animalium sequenti nocte comedunt clerici cum sale; sed sacerdos, qui in cratinum debet celebrare pro mortuo, non comedit de carnibus dictorum animalium usque post Missam. Faciunt autem praedicta, quia dicunt et tenent, quod licet remissio peccatorum fiat principaliter per sanguinem Christi, tamen non fierit dicta remissio peccatorum, nisi sanguis animalium praedictorum effunderetur, in peccatorum vivorum et mortuorum remissionem, quia Lex Moysi dicit, quod remissio peccatorum fit per effusionem sanguinis animalium brutorum mundorum et sine eo non fit peccatorum vivorum et mortuorum remissio; et Dominus dicit in Evangelio, quod ipse non venit solvere legem, sed adimplere, quam solvisset, si peccatorum remissio fieret sine effusione sanguinis animalium brutorum. Et de hoc etiam reprehendit eos Damascenus, dicens quod dicti Armeni accipientes de erroribus Judaeorum, Saracenorum, paganorum et aliorum errantium, de illis erroribus suam fidem composuerunt; et de dicta fide in concilio Manesguerdensi librum composuerunt, qui apud eos vocatur *Radix fidei.*

XLVI Item, quod dicti Armeni observant discretionem ciborum mundorum et immundorum animalium, secundum quod lex Moysi dicit; et licet aliqui ex Armenis comedant porcum, tamen secundum eos, si sacerdos comederet de porco, postea non posset expellere daemones de obsessis corporibus, quia, ut dicunt, Dominus expellens daemones de duobus hominibus, misit eos in porcos.

XLVII. Item, quando Armeni ieiunant diebus ieiuniorum institutis inter eos, dietis diebus non comedunt carnes nec pisces nec ova nec caseum nec butyrum nec lac nec oleum; quia dicunt, quod omnia ista sunt quaedam carnes; comedunt autem solum herbas, panem et vinum; possunt tamen comedere quoties volunt illis diebus quibus ieiunant. Dicunt etiam et praedicant, quod illi, qui in diebus ieiuniorum comedunt pisces, ova, caseum, butyrum et oleum, sunt maledicti et infideles et contra fidem constituti et sunt separata ab ovili Christi.

XLVIII. Item, Armeni dicunt et tenent, quod si Armeni committant semel quodcumque crimen, quibusdam exceptis, Ecclesia eorum potest absolvere eos quantum ad culpam et poenam de dictis criminibus, sed si aliquis postea committeret iterum dicta crimina, absolvi non posset per eorum Ecclesiam.

XLIX. Item dicunt, quod si aliquis eorum post baptismum accipiat primam et secundam uxorem, absolvi potest per eos, sed si accipiat tertiam vel quartam et deinceps, non potest absolvi per eorum Ecclesiam, quia dicunt, quod tale matrimonium fornicatio est et talem habent pro pagano, ita quod nec in fine eum communicant nec aducunt eum de domo sua ad sepeliendum per portam domus, sed frangunt parietem domus et per foramen parietis educunt corpus eius; nec Missam celebrant nec sepultura ecclesiastica eum sepeliunt, sed faciunt de eo sicut de pagano. Si tamen ille qui recipit tertiam uxorem, dum vivit eam dimittit sic, quod postea non revertatur ad eam, recipiunt eum ad poenitentiam et imponunt ei quindecim annos pro poenitentia sic, quod in dictis annis non comedat carnes, pisces et supradicta lacticinia; et si dictam poenitentiam perfecerit et postea moriatur, faciunt de eo sicut de christiano alio in vita et in morte.

L. Item, Armeni dicunt et tenent, quod si aliquis ante susceptionem Ordinis Sacri commiserit aliquod peccatum luxuriae carnalis exterioris, quod ille habet confiteri confessori dictum peccatum et deinde episcopus, qui Ordines facit, interrogat dictum confessorem, si est ille dignus ordinari; cui sacerdos respondet, quod non; et sic repellitur a suscipiendo Ordine Sacro. Si vero postquam ordinatus est, commiserit tale peccatum luxuriae, oportet quod si absolvi velit, confiteatur confessori suo; et tunc ille confessor deponit eum ab executione Ordinis; et si postea exequatur actus dicti Ordinis, dictus confessor dicit hoc episcopo, etiam in praesentia aliorum, et eum qua vel quo peccavit revelat. Mulieres etiam, cum quibus tales peccaverunt, iactant se dicendo: *Ego deposui talem sacerdotem;* ex quo contingit apud Armenos, quod multi sunt qui dicta peccata nolunt confiteri dum vivunt, ne repellantur a susceptione Sacrorum Ordinum; et si eos susceperint, ne postea deponantur ab Ordinis executione.

LI. Item, quod Armeni dicunt et tenent, quod ista peccata sunt irremissibilia nec eorum Ecclesia potest haec peccata remittere, quia Christus non dedit Ecclesiae potestatem quod talia peccata remittat, scilicet si aliquis peccatum luxuriae committat in ore hominis vel mulieris et si blasphemat Christum vel fidem christianam aut crucem; et tales blasphemos non reputant christianos nec ecclesiastica Sacramenta eis ministrant, dum vivunt nec quando moriuntur faciunt de eis sicut de christianis nec eorum filios reciperent ad baptismum, nisi convertantur et poenitentiam agant.

LII. Item, quod dicti Armeni dicunt et tenent, quod si aliquis semel commiserit peccatum adulterii, sodomiae, bestialitatis vel homicidii aut apostasiam a fide, faciendo se Saracenum vel Judaeum et etiam si aliquis dicat quod in Christo sunt duae naturae et una persona, potest absolvi per eorum Ecclesiam, non tamen debet communicari nisi in fine vitae suae. Et si quis commiserit dicta peccata vel etiam alia pluries, non potest absolvi per Ecclesiam, nisi prima vice; et si, postquam semel confessus fuerit et absolutus de aliquo peccato de praedictis, iterato committat dictum peccatum, prima absolutio non valet.

LIII. Item, quod dicti Armeni dicunt et tenent, quod si sacerdos habens uxorem, cum ipsa committat sodomiam, non peccat nec si hoc confiteatur deponitur, sed in hoc dimittitur conscientiae suae, quod confiteatur vel non confiteatur, si vult.

LIV. Item, quod inter Armenos catholicon et episcopi excommunicant Armenos sine omni culpa excommunicatorum et nulla monitione praemissa, ut volunt. Et dicunt, quod excommunicati per eos non possunt absolvi de aliquo peccato, nisi per catholicon vel episcopos, qui eos excommunicaverunt; si tamen vadant ad alium catholicon vel episcopos, alii catholicon subiectos possunt absolvi per eos a dicta excommunicatione et peccatis suis. Dicunt etiam et tenent, quod excommunicatis non debent ecclesiastica sacramenta ministrari. Et si aliquis excommunicatus moriatur, amici eius vadunt vel mittunt ad illum, qui eum excommunicavit et dant ei pecuniam vel alias res valentes pecuniam, prout conveniunt cum eo; et tunc excommunicans dat eis licentiam, quod ipsum sepeliant ecclesiastica sepultura. Qui faciunt pro eo illa, quae supra dicta sunt de animalibus; non tamen aliter absolvunt illum ab excommunicatione.

LV. Item, Armeni dicunt et tenent, quod excommunicationis sententia, etiam iuste lata, secundum Domini ordinationem, quia monitus non vult Ecclesiae oboedire nec se de peccato quod comsit emendare, non excidit a regno Dei, quia ita bene, excommunicatus sicut non excommunicatus vadit ad regnum Dei; sed fornicatio, adulterium, homicidium et si sacerdos accipiat secundam uxorem et si aliquis ex Armenis dicat esse in Christo duas naturas et duas operationes et unam personam, ista excludunt a regno Dei et non excommunicatio lata propter inoboedientiam Ecclesiae; unde Armeni parum vel nihil reputant excommunicationem valere.

LVI. Item, quod Armeni dicunt et tenent, quod si aliquis fuisset baptizatus in Ecclesia Armenorum et postea lapsus fuisset in haeresim vel in apostasiam a fide, faciendo se Saracenum vel Judaeum et deinde vellet reverti ad Ecclesiam Armenorum, non rebaptizatur, sed solum cum chrismate inungitur, nec aliter absolvitur; imponitur tamen ei, quod vadat ad locum illum, in quo commisit apostasiam a fide et ibi coram omnibus confiteatur peccatum suum et abneget illam perfidiam, quam commisit. Si tamen aliquis fuisset baptizatus in Ecclesia alicuius catholicon Armenorum et postea converteretur ad fidem Romanae

Ecclesiae vel Graecae, si postea vellet venire ad Ecclesiam primam, in qua fuerat prius baptizatus, illa Ecclesia sic baptizaret eum acsi nunquam fuisset baptizatus, sed semper fuisset Saracenus vel paganus. Si vero aliquis fuisset primo baptizatus in Ecclesia Romana vel Graeca et postea vellet venire ad Ecclesiam Armenorum, illa Ecclesia, ad quam veniret, baptizaret eum ac si nunquam baptizatus fuisset, sed semper fuisset paganus vel Saracenus. Et quia Armeni ideo dicunt quod baptizati in Ecclesia Romana vel Graeca, quando veniunt ad Ecclesiam Armenorum, rebaptizari debent, quia Ecclesia Romana et Graeca, ex eo quod dicunt duas naturas esse in Christo, fidem negaverunt et ex eo quia ponunt aquam in vino in Sacrificio, non habent aquam baptismi, quia aqua quae fluxit de latere Christi, non potest servire nisi sacramento baptismi, unde cum ponatur in Sacrificio per dictas Ecclesias, eaedem Ecclesiae non habent aquam baptismi, sine qua non potest fieri baptismus; ex eo etiam dictae Ecclesiae non habent baptismum, quia non habent verum Chrisma, sine quo verum baptisma non datur; et propter praedicta quia Ecclesia Latina et Graeca non habent verum baptismum, sed solum Ecclesia Armena dictum baptismum verum habet, quia contraria dictis Ecclesiis tenet et habet; et ideo Ecclesia Armena baptizat baptizatos in Ecclesia Latina vel Graeca, quando veniunt ad eam.

LVII. Item, Armeni dicunt et tenent, quod verum chrisma sic conficitur, quod habent diversos flores aromaticos et alios quos invenire possunt in die Ramispalmarum et illos decoquunt in vino et deinde dictum vinum accipiunt et per quatuor dies ante diem Coenae ponunt dictum vinum in oleo et decoquunt insimul et astant tunc multi episcopi et sacerdotes, dicentes multas orationes, dum haec decoctio fit. Et deinde die Coenae accipitur unus fiasco de dicto oleo et in ipso fiascone ponit catholicon balsamum et postea catholicon celebrat Missam; et quando catholicon elevat Corpus Domini, unus episcopus qui astat ei, elevat dictum flasconem et catholicon dicit orationes. Et deinde de dicto flascone ponitur in diversis vasis, quae stant ibi iuxta altare et sic verum chrisma conficitur solum per catholicon modo praedicto; et sine tali chrismate non potest dari verus baptismus. Unde contigit apud eos, quod pueri portati ad baptismum, quia sacerdos non habet de dicto chrismate vel illi qui puerum portaverunt, nolunt tantum dare pro chrismate quantum sacerdos vellet, frequenter moriuntur sine baptismate; de quibus pueris dicunt Armeni, quod in die Iudicii baptizabuntur de sanguine qui fluxit de latere Christi, quia, ut dicunt, quando Christus moriebatur in cruce, luna descendit et accepit sanguinem Christi, qui adhuc manet in luna; et ex hoc apparet aliqua nigredo in luna, quae prius non apparebat; in die autem Iudicii effluet dictus sanguis de luna, de quo baptizabuntur dicti parvuli, ut sic possint intrare in caelorum <regnum>.

LVIII. Item, quod Armeni dicunt et tenent, quod ad hoc, quod sit baptismus verus, ista tria requiruntur, scilicet aqua, chrisma modo praedicto factum et Eucharistia; ita quod, si aliquis baptizaret in aqua aliquem, dicendo: *Ego te baptizo in nomine Patris, et Filii, et Spiritus Sancti. Amen,* et postea non inungeretur dicto chrismate, non esset baptismus. Si etiam non daretur ei Eucharistiae sacramentum, baptizatus non esset. Et etiam apud eos non baptizantur pueri antequam habeant octo dies. Et species sacramenti Eucharistiae liquefiunt in aqua vel vino et ponuntur in ore primum baptizati et sic accipiunt Eucharistiae sacramentum et tunc dicuntur vere esse baptizati. Quae tria si non fierent, Armeni non reputarent puerum vere baptizatum. Dicunt etiam, quod pueri non baptizantur in peccatorum remissionem, quia nullum peccatum habent; adulti vero baptizantur in peccatorum remissionem, non quia in aqua baptizantur, sed quia dicto chrismate inunguntur et accipiunt Eucharistiae sacramentum.

LIX. Item, quod Armeni diversimode baptizant et quantum ad materiam et quantum ad formam baptismi. Quantum ad materiam quidem, quia aliqui, licet pauci, baptizant in vino puro, alii vero in lacte, alii vero communiter in aqua. Quantum vero ad formam, nulla forma baptismi certa est apud eos, sed quilibet episcopus vel presbyter ordinat sibi formam, in qua baptizet et modum baptizandi tenet quem vult. Aliqui enim ex eis, qui in aqua baptizant, non nominant, dum baptizant, tres personas divinas dicendo: *Baptizetur iste in nomine Patris, et Filii, et Spiritus Scancti;* sed dum baptizatum in aqua lavant, dicunt evangelium ab illo loco: *Venit Jesus a Galilaea in Jordanem ad Joannem,* usque ad illum locum: *et vox facta est dicens: Hic est Filiius meus.* Alii vero, dum baptizatum lavant, dicunt: *Vox Domini super aguas; Deus maiestatis intonuit; Dominus super aquas multas.* Alii vero dum baptizatum lavant, dicunt antiphonam, scilicet: ' *Dum erant Apostoli in caenaculo, repente venit sonitus de caelo tamquam spiritus vehementis cum magna voce et accendit eos in igne, sine ardore.* Dicunt etiam aliam antiphonam: *Repente descendit Spiritus Sanctus in similitudinem glorian super Apostolos*; et aliam etiam, quae talis est: '*Benedictio in excelsis Spiritus Sancti procedentis a Padre, per quem inebriati sunt Apostoli vino immortali et invitaverunt terram ad caelum*'. Illi vero, qui baptizant in vino, dum lavant illum qui baptizatur, dicunt: '*Ego te lavo in vino, ut sis fortis et ne patiaris frigus*'. Illorum vero, qui baptizant in lacte non exprimitur aliqua forma. Alii vero, dum lavant baptizandos, dicunt quod ipsi vellent committere turpia cum matre pueri qui baptizatur. Aliqui etiam ex Armenis, quando ponunt baptizandum in aqua, dicunt: '*Baptizetur talis in nomine Patris, et Filii, et Spiritus Sancti* et deinde dum baptizandum lavant, dicunt iterum eadem verba; et deinde quando extrabunt de aqua, dicunt eadem verba; et deinde inungunt baptizandum cum chrismate in oculis, in auribus, in fronte in naribus, in ore, in et sub axellis, in genu et sub genu, in pedibus, in soleis, dicendo certa verba et postea baptizatum communicant de sacrificio altaris. Et sic, ut dicunt, homo vere et plene est baptizatus et aliter non.

LX. Item, quod si aliquis Armenus baptizatus in aqua vel vino aut lacte modis supradictis, etiam si, dum baptizatur in aqua, dicatur: *Baptizetur iste in nomine Patris et Filii et Spiritus Sancti,* transeat ad Ecclesiam Latinam vel Graecam et postea revertatur ad primam Ecclesiam, ita rebaptizatur ac si paganus semper fuisset; si vero de Ecclesia unius catholicon transeat ad ecclesiam alterius catholicon, ille catholicon, ad cuius ecclesiam vadit, facit eum negare fidem illius catholicon, qui eum baptizavit et chrismavit eum modo supradicto, dicens quod chrisma alterius catholicon nihil valet, nisi suum; non tamen rebaptizat eum, excepto catholicon Armeniae Minoris, qui baptizatos et chrismatos in ecclesiis catholicon Maioris Armeniae venientes ad ecclesiam Minoris Armeniae, rebaptizat et chrismat modo supradicto.

LXI. Item Armeni dicunt, quod virtute sacramenti baptismi baptizatus efficitur membrum Ecclesiae et potest participare Sacramentis et efficitur christianus et post finale iudicium, nisi aliud obsistat, intrabit in regnum caelorum.

LXII. Item, Armeni dicunt et tenent, quod licet in eorum Ordinario antiquo dicatur, quod per baptismum datur remissio peccatorum, ipsi tamen hoc sic exposuerunt, quod hoc veritatem non habet de pueris, qui in aetate puerili baptizantur infra aetatem duodecim annorum, quia tales reputant innocentes et sine peccato; quia ipsi Armeni pro maximo peccato habent peccatum luxuriae, quod committere non possunt tales pueri; sed de illis qui baptizantur postquam peccata luxuriae commiserunt, dicunt quod tales baptizantur in remissionem peccatorum. Tenent etiam dicti Armeni, quod illi, qui non commiserunt peccatum luxuriae, sunt virgines et innocentes, etiam si non baptizati decederent.

LXIII. Item, apud Armenos utriusque Armeniae non datur Sacramentum Confirmationis, quia ut dicunt, illi qui eis fidem praedicaverunt a principio, tale Sacramentum eis non dederunt; et quamvis Apostoli miserint Petrum et Joannem ad illos, qui baptizati fuerant in Samaria per Philippum, ut imponerent eis manus et acciperent Spiritum Sanctum, quod ad Sacramentum Confirmationis pertinere videtur, dicunt tamen Armeni, quod illi, qui baptizati fuerant per Philippum, non acceperant verum baptismum, quia Philippus solum erat diaconus et non presbyter vel episcopus, quia presbyter et episcopus solum possunt dare verum baptismum; et ideo missi fuerunt dicti duo Apostoli ad eos, ut verum baptismum et Spiritum Sanctum acciperent. Dicunt etiam dicti Armeni, quod eunuchus baptizatus a Philippo, in tali baptismo non accepit Spiritum Sanctum, sed postquam Philippus arreptus fuit ab eo, Spiritus Sanctus venit super eunuchum.

LXIV. Item, catholicon Minoris Armeniae dicit, quod Sacramentum Confirmationis nihil valet et si valet aliquid, ipse dedit licentiam presbyteris suis, ut idem Sacramentum conferant.

LXV. Item, Armeni dicunt et tenent, quod illa inunctio cum chrismate facta in novem locis, de qua supradictum est, valet christianis, dum vivunt, pro omnibus inunctionibus quae fiunt per Ecclesiam Latinam; unde apud eos non est Sacramentum Confirmationis nec Extremae Unctionis nec, quando consecrantur presbyteri vel episcopi, inunguntur eorum manus vel capita; sed quando episcopi vel presbyteri sunt mortui, portantur ante altare et ibi eorum capita et frontes ac manus dexterae inunguntur et tunc populus venit et osculatur manum dexteram praedictorum et faciunt oblationes suas ac si primam Missam haberet celebrare; et postea adducuntur ad ostium ecclesiae animalia munda cooperta pannis sericis et modo supradicto occiduntur et postea comeduntur.

LXVI. Item, omnes Armeni communiter dicunt et tenent, quod per haec verba posita in eorum Canone Missae, quando dicuntur per sacerdotem; ' *Accepit panem el gratias agens, fregit, dedit suis sanctis electis et recumbentibus discipulis, dicens: Accipite et manducate ex hoc omnes: Hoc est Corpus meum, quod pro vobis et multis distribuitur, in remissionem peccatorum. Similiter et calicem accipiens, benedixit et fregit, gratias egit, bibit, dedit suis electis sanctis et recumbentibus discipulis dicens: Accipte, bibite ex hoc omnes: Hic est Sanguis meus novi testamenti, qui pro vobis et multis effunditur, in remissionem peccatorum,* non conficitur nec ipsi conficere intendunt Corpus et Sanguinem Christi, sed solum dicunt dicta verba recitative, recitando scilicet quod Dominus fecit, quando Sacramentum instituit. Et post dicta verba dicit sacerdos multas orationes positas in eorum Canone et post dictas orationes venit ad locum, ubi sic in eorum Canone dicitur: ' *Adoramus, supplicamus et petimus a te, benigne Deus, mitte in nobis et in hoc propositum donum coëssentialem tibi Spiritum Sanctum, per quem panem benedictum Corpus veraciter efficies domini nostri et salvatoris Jesu Christi*'. Et dicta verba dicit sacerdos ter. Deinde dicit sacerdos super calicem et vinum benedictum: ' *Sanguinem veracite efficies domini nostri salvatoris Jesu Christi* '; et per haec verba credunt, quod conficiantur Corpus Christi et Sanguis. Diversum etiam ritum habent dicti Armeni in celebrando Missam, quia quidam eorum in altari ponunt duos calices, in quibus ponunt panem et vinum; et quidam ponunt solum unum, in quo ponunt vinum; et calices apud eos sunt vel terrei vel lignei. Et quidam celebrant Missam in communibus vestibus et quidam induuntur sacris vestibus; et quidam celebrant populo praesente et quidam excluso populo et clausis ianuis. Sacerdos celebrans, solus intrat ecclesiam et exit et penitus non ostendit populo corpus Domini; et adhuc in pluribus locis fit isto modo, quod celebrant sub ianua clausa, quousque sacerdos dicit: *Respicite;* quando scilicet elevat sacramentum, ut populus videat; et tunc aperiuntur ianuae ecclesiae.

LXVII. Item, quod Armeni non dicunt, quod post dicta verba consecrationis panis et vini sit facta transubstantiatio panis et vini in verum Corpus Christi et Sanguinem, quod natum fuit de Virgine Maria et passum et resurrexit, sed tenent, quod illud sacramentum sit exemplar vel similitudo aut figura veri

Corporis et Sanguinis Domini; et hoc specialiter aliqui magistri Armenorum dixerunt, videlicet quod non erat ibi Corpus Christi verum et Sanguis, sed exemplar et similitudo eius. Dicunt etiam, quod quando Christus Sacramentum instituit, non transubstantiavit panem et vinum in corpus suum et sanguinem, sed solummodo instituit exemplar et similitudinem corporis et sanguinis sui; propter quod ipsi Sacramentum altaris non vocant corpus et sanguinem Domini, sed *hostiam* vel *sacrificium* vel *communionem*. Quidam etiam magister vocatus Narces habet in suis libris expressum, quod quando sacerdos dicit haec verba: ' *Hoc est corpus meum*', tunc est ibi corpus Christi mortuum; sed quando sacerdos dicit: *Per quem*, ut propositum est, ibi est corpus Christi vivum; non tamen expressit, si erat verum corpus Christi ibi vel similitudo eius. Et quod etiam Armeni illud quod ponitur in eorum Canone Missae: ' *Per quem panis benedictus efficitur verum corpus Christi* ', sic ly *verum corpus Christi,* exponunt, quia efficitur ibi vera similitudo et exemplar corporis et sanguinis Christi. Unde et Damascenus propter hoc reprehendens eos dixit, quod ducenti tunc anni erant, quod Armeni perdiderunt omnia Sacramenta et quod illa Sacramenta quae habebant, non erant eis tradita ab Apostolis vel ab Ecclesia Graeca vel Latina, sed ipsi, ut voluerant, sibi Sacramenta confinxerant.

LXVIII. Item, Armeni dicunt et tenent, quod si presbyter vel episcopus ordinatus committat fornicationem, etiam in secreto, perdit potestatem conficiendi et ministrandi omnia Sacramenta quae pertinent ad episcopum vel presbyterum; et talia Sacramenta per eos confecta nullam efficaciam vel virtutem habent. Si autem publicum sit, quod fornicati fuerunt, nullus Armenus Sacramenta confecta per eos acciperet, quia credunt, quod talia Sacramenta nullam virtutem vel efficaciam habent, eo quod tales fornicatores perdiderunt potestatem Sacramenta conficiendi et administrandi; dicunt tamen, quod bonus laicus et fidelis Eucharistiam confectam per episcopum vel presbyterum habentem potestatem conficiendi Sacramentum Eucharistiae, eam aliis ministrare potest.

LXIX. Item, dicti Armeni dicunt, quod si episcopus vel presbyter committat fornicationem vel quamcumque aliam speciem luxuriae, secrete vel publice, perdit potestatem conficiendi et ministrandi Sacramenta quae ad eum pertinent; si vero efficiatur haereticus vel apostata a fide, ut si efficiatur Saracenus vel Judaeus vel committat quodcumque aliud crimen, ut homicidium, periurium et sic de aliis criminibus, dictam potestatem conficiendi et ministrandi Sacramenta non perdit, sed sufficit quod de talibus peccatis poeniteat, sive dicta peccata commiserit publice sive occulte.

LXX. Item, Armeni non dicunt nec tenent, quod sacramentum Eucharistiae digne susceptum operetur in suscipiente peccatorum remissionem vel poenarum debitarum peccato relaxationem vel quod per ipsum detur gratia Dei vel eius augmentum, sed solum dicunt, quod effectus Sacramenti Eucharistiae sunt isti, scilicet quod ille qui recipit hoc Sacramentum, Christus manet in eo, quia scilicet Corpus Christi intrat in eius corpus et in ipsum convertitur, sicut et alia alimenta convertuntur in alimentato. Et quia Eucharistia manet in suscipiente, dicunt quod presbyter qui accipit Corpus Christi, non debet phlebotomari postea per triduum; et quia quidam presbyter contrarium fecit, exivit de phlebotomia sanguis et ignis. Dicunt etiam Armeni, quod effectus Eucharistiae sunt, ut custodiatur accipiens a fulgure et grandine et ab aliis aeris nocivis impressionibus et ab infirmitatibus coporis et talibus malis corporalibus suis vel carorum suorum. Et idem dicunt quoad istas poenalitates corporales de Sacramento Poenitentiae, quod scilicet homines per dictum Sacramentum a talibus poenalitatibus custodiuntur.

LXXI. Item, quod sexcenti duodecim anni sunt, quod concilium supradictum fuit celebratum per Armenos in civitate Manesguerdensi et ibi patriarcha Surianorum, catholicon, episcopi ac magistri Armenorum determinaverunt, quod in Sacrificio altaris non deberet misceri aqua in vino; et nihilominus determinaverunt ibi, quod illi qui miscent aquam in vino in Sacramento altaris, non habent verum baptismum, quia illa aqua, quae fluxit de latere Christi in cruce, non potest servire nisi Sacramento baptismi; et ideo qui aquam ponunt in vino, perdiderunt Sacramentum baptismi. Determinaverunt etiam in dicto concilio, quod si aqua in sacrificio altaris poneretur, quod illud Sacramentum nullum esset, quia Dominus post confectionem Sacramenti Eucharistiae dixit: *Non bibam de hoc genimine vitis,* et ita, solum genimen vitis debet poni in sacrificio et non aqua. In quo etiam concilio anathematizaverunt illos, qui ponebant vel ponerent aquam in dicto sacrificio; et in tantum hoc detestantur, quod si in aliqua Armenorum ecclesia celebretur Missa, in qua misceatur aqua in vino, aliqua pars tecti ecclesiae discooperitur, ut radius solis in ea intrare possit, per cuius introitum consecratio dictae ecclesiae tollitur et postea antequam aliquis Armenus in dieta ecclesia Missam celebret, oportet quod dicta ecclesia reconcilietur.

LXXII. Item, Armeni antiqui dixerunt et tenuerunt, quod nullus non ordinatus in presbyterum, quantumcumque esset bonae vitae, poterat conficere Sacramentum Eucharistiae; et quod illi, qui erant in presbyteros ordinati, si malae vitae essent, non poterant dictum Sacramentum conficere; sed boni presbyteri hoc facere poterant et non alii. Armeni vero moderni dicunt, quod boni et mali presbyteri, dummodo non dimiserint legem Armenorum nec effecti fuerint de lege Ecclesiae Latinae vel Graecae nec commiserint peccata de quibus supra dictum est, possunt conficere dictum Sacramentum. Sed illi presbyteri, qui dimiserunt legem Armenorum vel facti sunt de lege Ecclesiae Graecae vel Latinae, quia eam dimittendo effecti sunt haeretici, non possunt conficere dictum Sacramentum.

LXXIII. Item, Armeni habent in quodam canone, quod si aliquis fuisset baptizatus in quibuscumque ecclesiis, quae tenerent quod in Christo sunt duae naturae et una persona et vellet a presbyteris Armenorum accipere Eucharistiae Sacramentum, idem Sacramentum non daretur ei per dictos presbyteros, nisi prius abnegaret baptismum quod prius acceperat et malediceret illos, qui dicunt duas naturas esse in Christo et qui miscent aquam in vino in Sacrificio; quibus factis, rebaptizant eum modo Armenorum et tunc dant ei Eucharistiae Sacramentum per eos modo Armenorum confectum; et quod presbyteri Armenorum, dum celebrant Missam clausis ianuis ecclesiae, secundum quod supra dictum est, maledicunt illos, qui dicunt duas naturas esse in Christo et qui miscent aquam in Sacrificio et qui aliquam reverentiam faciunt imaginibus Dei vel Sanctorum.

LXXIV. Item, quod apud Armenos Maioris Armeniae non sit imago Crucifixi nec aliae imagines tenentur Sanctorum.

LXXV. Item, quod quidam magister Armenorum, cum venisset ad quemdam locum ubi fiebat solemnitas et sacerdos elevasset Eucharistiae Sacramentum, ut videretur a populo, dictus magister maledixit eidem sacerdoti dicens, quod mysterium fidei in secreto debebat teneri et non populo ostendi et quod, ostendendo dictum Sacramentum, sacerdos videatur dicere populo: 'Non timeatis, quia unum frustum panis est hoc sacramentum'.

LXXVI. Item, quod fuerunt Bononiae tres Armeni, qui prius fuerant baptizati in forma Armenorum et postea fuerunt baptizati in forma Ecclesiae Latinae (nempe sub conditione, si baptismo non essent rite abluti, ut ex litteris pontificiis constat), qui homines cum postea venissent apud Florentiam, dum Armeni interrogaverunt eos, an fuissent balneati, vocantes balneationem baptismum receptum in Ecclesia Latina; qui cum respondissent eis, quod sint, dixerunt eis, quod abnegarent dictam balneationem. Quod cum facere nollent, tantum verberaverunt eos, quod unus ex eis post paucos dies decessit; alios vero duos tamdiu in carcere detinuerunt, quousque dictam balneationem abnegarent, dicendo quod dictam balneationem reputabant ac si unus canis minxisset super eos; et fuerunt per eos, ut creditur, rebaptizati secundum modum Armenorum; alioquin talibus non darent Eucharistiae Sacramentum etiam in fine, quantumcumque peterent.

LXXVII. Item, cum quidam clerici et laici Armeni fuissent baptizati in forma Ecclesiae Latinae, catholicon Minoris Armeniae eos fecit capi et dehonestari, radendo totaliter eorum capita et medietatem barbae et scindendo vestes eorum et postea in carcerem poni et cogebat eos Sacramentum Baptisimi, quod acceperant in forma Ecclesiae Romanae, abnegare; et quia facere noluerunt, diu fecit eos in carcere detineri.

LXXVIII. Item, quod cum duo archiepiscopi, dubitantes an essent vere ordinati et baptizati per Armenos, venissent ad catholicon qui nunc est Minoris Armeniae, dictus catholicon vocavit praedictos archiepiscopos et inhibuit eis hoc: primo, quod non celebrarent Missam Latinam, sed Armenorum antiquam Missam; secundo, praecepit eis, quod non servarent ieiunia Ecclesiae Romanae, sed antiqua ieiunia Armenorum; tertio, praecepit, quod non baptizarent aliquem, qui dubitaret de suo baptismo et veniret ad eos ad petendum verum baptismum, sed ut dicerent eis, quod baptismus Armenorum est melior, quam baptismus Ecclesiae Romanae; quarto, inhibuit eis, ne facerent populum suum Armenorum latinum, quia dicebat ille dictus catholicon, quod melius erat quod populus suus sicut Armenus vadat ad Infernum, quam si fierent Latini et irent omnes ad paradisum; quinto praecepit eis, quod non docerent pueros armenos nec linguam nec litteram latinam, quia quando addiscerent litteram latinam, amitterent linguam Armenorum. Et ad testimonium et confirmationem horum dictorum est hoc, quod in eodem anno supradictus catholicon consecravit sex episcopos armenos et accepit ab eis litteram publicam, quod ipsi non darent pueros de partibus suis ad addiscendum litteram latinam nec dimitterent aliquem praedicatorem latinum, qui praedicaret veritatem Sanctae Romanae Ecclesiae in dioecesi et provincia sua. Item quemlibet episcopum, quem ipse consecrat, facit anathematizare illos Armenos qui volunt fieri veri catholici et oboedientes Ecclesiae Romanae. Sexto, inhibuit eis, quod non praedicarent papam Romanum caput esse Ecclesiae in Orientalibus partibus, sed ipse se dicit et facit papam in partibus Orientalibus a fine maris usque ad magnum imperium Tartarorum. Et multa alia inconvenientia verba et errorem sapientia locutus fuit et haec omnia inhibuit eis dictus catholicon; et quia noluerunt ei oboedire in praedictis, gravem persecutionem contra eos fecit, propter quod unus ex eis post annum cum dimidio ivit ad insulam Cypri et ibi audivit quod dictus catholicon, consentiente rege Armeniae, illos quos ipsi et aliqui alii Latini baptizaverant vel ordinaverant sub conditione in forma Ecclesiae Romanae, capi fecit et aliquos sacerdotes ex eis degradavit et in duro carcere regis posuit; alios vero incarceravit et adhuc sunt carcerati et eorum bona et possessiones fuerunt confiscatae et aliis venditae.

LXXIX. Item, quod presbyteri et episcopi Armenorum imponunt poenitentiam illis Armenis, qui veniunt ut baptizentur in Ecclesia Graeca vel Latina, per aliquos annos, ut scilicet ieiunent modo Armenorum. Modus autem talis est, quod in dicto tempore non debent comedere carnes, pisces, lac, caseum vel ova; possunt tamen quoties volunt in die comedere. Illis vero Armenis, qui accipiunt Eucharistiae Sacramentum in Ecclesia Graeca vel Latina, imponunt poenitentiam quinque annorum, ut scilicet ieiunent per dictum tempus modo supradicto.

LXXX. Item, quod apud Armenos in Quadragesima, quam incipiunt dominica in quinquagesima, non celebratur Missa in ecclesiis, nisi in die sabbati et dominica; nec dicitur aliis septimanis anni, in quibus Armeni ieiunant. Magis autem celebrant Missas in die sabbati quam in aliis diebus dictis temporibus, quia communiter omnia festa, quae veniunt in septimana, celebrant in die sabbati, exceptis festis Assumptionis B. Mariae et Exaltationis sanctae Crucis, quae festa celebrant in die dominica. Alio vero tempore anni communiter in ecclesiis non celebrant nisi dictis duobus diebus in septimana, et tunc etiam ducunt animalia ad ostium ecclesiae et occidunt modis supradictis.

LXXXI. Item, quod apud Armenos populus non communicat nisi in vigilia Epiphaniae et in die <Epiphaniae>; ita quod illi, qui ieiunaverunt per septimanam ante dictam vigiliam, in dicta vigilia, vel nocte sequenti, communicant; et ibi anathematizant omnes illos, qui faciunt festum Nativitatis Domini XXV die decembris. In sequenti vero die faciunt festum Epiphaniae, et tunc illi de populo qui volunt, communicant; etiam illi, qui non ieiunaverunt dictam septimanam; communicant etiam aliqui in die Coenae et in Sabbato sancto.

LXXXII. Item, quod quando aliqui communicare debent per sacerdotem, fit confessio generalis, dicendo genera peccatorum, non descendendo ad aliquod peccatum singulare; et postea populus reiterat dictam confessionem; in secreto tamen raro vel nunquam aliquis Armenus confitetur sacerdoti sua peccata; et si confitetur, non dicit quod hoc vel illud singulare peccatum commiserit, sed dicit, quod diabolus dictum peccatum fecit vel quod ad suggestionem alterius hominis dictum peccatum fecit. Dimittunt autem peccata sua confiteri secrete et singulariter, quia sacerdotes eorum peccata revelarent et multum graves poenitentias eis imponerent; propter quod communiter Armeni non confitentur nisi in genere peccata sua. Facta autem dicta generali confessione per populum, sacerdos dicit vel: '*Ego dimitto vobis peccata vestra*' vel: *Deus dimittat vobis '*; et aliqui dicunt: *Ego dimitto vobis peccata vestra in terra et Deus dimittat vobis in caelo*'. Dicti autem sacerdotes dicunt, quod nisi dictas poenitentias compleverint, non debent communicare in vita praesenti nec ingredientur in regnum Dei; et erunt exclusi a gratia et benedictione Dei. Et apud Armenos nullam certam formam habent presbyteri et sacerdotes absolvendi subiectos eorum a peccatis suis. Item, quod dicti Armeni dicunt et tenent, quod dicta generalis confessio sufficit ad remissionem peccatorum et absolutionem; nec oportet quod secrete et in singulari aliquis confiteatur peccata sua sacerdoti; dicta etiam absolutio generalis valet ad peccatorum absolutionem, etiam si contritio non praecesserit.

LXXXIII. Item, Armeni infirmi graviter, quando dicitur eis quod morti appropinquant, ipsi vel eorum amici petunt communionem et eam faciunt portari; et quandoque contingit, quod quando multum debiles sunt, sacerdotes ponunt in ore eorum communionem; et quando sunt multum proximi morti, faciunt sacerdotes de communione signum crucis super os eorum et sic reportant communionem.

LXXXIV. Item, Armeni dicunt et tenent, quod catholicon, episcopi et presbyter Armenorum eamdem et aequalem potestatem habent ligandi vel solvendi, quantam et qualem habuit Petras Apostolas, cui a Domino dictum est: ' *Quodcumque ligaveris super terram, erit ligatum et in caelis; et quodcumque solveris super terram, erit solutum et in caelis*'; nec quoad hoc minorem potestatem habent presbyteri Armenorum, quam eorum catholicon et episcopi.

LXXXV. Item, Armeni dicunt et tenent, quod usque ad concilium Nicaenum Romanus Pontifex non habuit potestatem maiorem, quam alii patriarchae; sed tunc de voluntate dicti concilii fuit orditum, quod dictus Romanus Pontifex haberet potestatem super alios patriarchas. Quam potestatem habuerunt Romani Pontifices usque ad concilium Chalcedonense; sed quia in dicto concilio, ad instantiam b. Leonis papae congregato, fuit determinatum, quod in Cristo erant duae naturae et una persona, Romani Pontifices perdiderunt dictam potestatem et omnes illi, qui dicto concilio consenserunt; et ex tunc illa plena potestas ligandi vel solvendi, quam Christus Ecclesiae in persona b. Petri <contulerat>, apud solos Armenos remansit; et hoc etiam Armeni determinaverunt in supradicto concilio Manesguerdensi, quod congregatum fuit ibi de mandato cuiusdam Saraceni, nepotis Machometi.

LXXXVI. Item, Armeni dicunt et tenent, quod post concilium Chalcedonense Romanus Pontifex non babet plus de potestate super subiectos suos, quam ille qui praeest Nestorianis super Nestorianos vel ille qui praeest Graecis super

Graecos. Dicunt etiam ulterius, quod papa scit quod potest et Armeni sciunt quod possunt.

LXXXVII. Item, quod rex Armenorum interrogavit catholicon Minoris Armeniae, an si papa excommunicaret eum, reputaret se excommunicatum; qui respondit quod non, quia papa nihil habet facere de eo nec ipse accepit aliquid a papa. Rex tamen dixit ei, quod si papa mandaret ei, quod dictum catholicon deponeret, ipse deponeret eum.

LXXXVIII. Item, catholicon Armenorum hoc modo eliguntur, instituuntur et confirmantur et potestatem pertinentem ad catholicon accipiunt et deponuntur et aliter puniuntur; quia catholicon Columbarum et catholicon Dehactamar viventes eligunt aliquem de gente ipsorum, quem volunt et postea consecrant eum in catholicon; non tamen utitur hac potestate, quousque mortuus fuit ille catholicon qui eum elegit. Postquam autem mortuus est dictus catholicon primus, sequens catholicon vadit ad imperatorem Tartarorum, qui est paganus, et ab ipso confirmatur in catholicon; et ut confirmetur per eum, exigitur ab eo pecunia, quantum solvere potest. Qui modus eligendi et confirmandi catholicon introductus fuit in Ecclesia Maioris Armeniae per Saporem regem Persarum, paganum, qui colebat ignem et durat usque nunc. Qua confirmatione facta per dictum regem, idem rex dat litteras suas, quod episcopi et subiecti ei oboediant, quia est confirmatus per eum; et quod dent ei certas quantitates pecuniae et postea annuatim alias; et omnes presbyteri dant ei ad minus valorem unius floreni annuatim et de quolibet facto christianorum et subiectorum habet annuatim valorem ad minus sex grossorum argenti; et dictus catholicon dicto regi quolibet anno habet dare certam summam pecuniae, quam si non daret vel aliud crimen committeret, dictus rex deponit eum et secundum quantitatem criminis commissi per eum punit eum etiam ad mortem. Catholicon vero Armeniae Minoris sic fit: quia mortuo catholicon, rex Armeniae convocat episcopos quos vult et illi eligunt tres episcopos Minoris Armeniae in catholicon et praesentant eos regi; qui rex coram quolibet electorum praedictorum flectit genua; et deinde ille de dictis electis, qui plus de pecunia dederit regi, per regem constituitur catholicon et confirmatur per hoc, quod rex imponit anulum in digito manus eius. Et iste catholicon, qui nunc est, dedit pro confirmatione sua dicto regi quinquaginta millia grossorum vel valorem ipsorum et quolibet anno dat ei viginti millia grossorum vel valorem. Dictus autem rex potest deponere dictum catholicon et aliter punire, quando vult; et apud Armenos catholicon, episcopi et presbyteri nullum Ordinem alicui dant, nisi interveniente pecunia nec chrisma nec aliquod aliud Sacramentum, sed omnia talia sunt venialia apud eos.

LXXXIX. Item, imperator Maioris Armeniae, quando confirmat dictos catholicon, dicit eis: ' *Eatis et faciatis officium secundum fidem vestram, et mandamus, quod possitis benedicere et maledicere et ligare et solvere, secundum fidem vestram, prout vobis videbitur, et volumus, quod christiani qui sunt sub vobis, oboediant vobis et si oboedire nollent, volumus quod illi, qui praesunt tetras, eos cogant vel puniant,* et de hoc dat ei privilegium. Et eodem modo fit de rege Armeniae Maioris de catholicon Minoris Armeniae et rex Minoris Armeniae eligit episcopos et presbyteros, accepta pecunia ab eis; et postea illos electos in episcopos mittit ad catholicon, ut consecrentur per eum et presbyteros ad episcopos, ut ordinentur per eos; qui etiam episcopi et presbyteri ordinantur per catholicon et per episcopos pro pecunia. Eo autem ipso quod sunt consecrati vel ordinati, a Deo immediate post consecrationem accipiunt potestatem ligandi et solvendi consimilem illi, quam Christus dedit b. Petro Apostolo; et tantam habent potestatem presbyteri, sicut episcopi et catholicon.

XC. Item, Armeni dicunt et tenent, quod potestas illa, quam Christus dedit b. Petro, dicendo ei ' *Quodcumque ligaveris super terram etc*', sunt solum data personae Petri et pro ipso solo, ita quod haec potestas non transivit ad aliquem eius successorem.

XCI. Item, quod Armeni dicunt et tenent, quod generalis potestas super totam Ecclesiam Christi non fuit data b. Petro nec successoribus eius a Christo, sed potestas fuit eis data per concilium Nicaenum, quam tamen potestatem postea successores Petri perdiderunt.

XCII. Item, quod apud Armenos non sunt nisi tres Ordines, scilicet acolytathus, diaconatus et presbyteratus; quos ordines conferunt episcopi, promissa vel accepta pecunia. Et eodem modo dicti Ordines presbyteratus et diaconatus confirmantur, scilicet per manus impositionem, dicendo quaedam verba, hoc solummodo mutato, quod in ordinatione diaconi exprimitur Ordo diaconatus et in ordinatione presbyteri Ordo presbyteratus. Nullus autem episcopus apud eos potest ordinare alium episcopum, nisi solus catholicon; qui catholicon tenet penes se pontificale, ubi continetur modus consecrandi episcopum. Dictus autem catholicon nullum in episcopum consecrat, nisi data vel promissa pecunia, secundum facultates consecrandi in episcopum vel valorem episcopatus. Et in Maiori Armenia consecrantes episcopos, presbyteros, diaconos vel acolythos, in communibus vestibus stant, dum praedicta faciunt et etiam ordinandi.

XCIII. Item, quod quando aliquis est ordinatus in diaconum, episcopus dat ei licentiam, quod contrahat matrimonium cum virgine; quo matrimonio contracto, ministrat in dicto Ordine et potest etiam stante matrimonio promoveri in sacerdotem; sed si existens diaconus accipiat secundam uxorem, postea non promovetur ad sacerdotium.

XCIV. Item, in Armenia Maiori, quando aliquis ordinatur in diaconum, non datur ei liber evangeliorum nec stola sub certa forma verborum; nec, quando aliquis ordinatur in presbyterum, datur ei calix cum vino et patena cum pane sub certa forma verborum, quibus utitur Romana Ecclesia; nec inunguntur ei manus; nec, quando aliquis ordinatur in episcopum, ponitur liber evangeliorum in cervice et in spatulis eius; nec caput nec manus ei inunguntur chrismate, ut fit in Ecclesia Romana. Catholicon etiam Maioris Armeniae soli consecrant episcopos, non assistentibus eis aliis episcopis.

XCV. Item quod catholicon Minoris Armeniae dedit potestatem cuidam presbytero, ut posset ordinare in diaconos quos vellet de subiectis; cum tamen apud Armenos Maioris Armeniae nullus possit ordinare aliquem diaconum vel presbyterum, nisi solus episcopus.

XCVI. Item, catholicon Minoris Armeniae, quando vult consecrare episcopos, induit se vestibus sacris; ipse tamen solus dictam consecrationem facit; si et aliqui episcopi sint ibi praesentes propter honorem eius, non tamen cum eo consecrant episcopum, sed solum assistunt in Missa, quando celebrat catholicon, sicut Cardinales quando papa celebrat; nec tenent librum pontificalem nec orationes dicunt, quae dicuntur per episcopos assistentes in consecratione episcoporum.

XCVII. Item, quod catholicon Armenorum conveniunt cum episcopis eis subiectis, qui non per successionem veniunt, de certa quantitate pecuniae annuatim ei danda; quam si non solvunt, deponit eos et consecrat alium episcopum in loco eius et cum suis litteris scribit populo eius, quod ipse primum episcopum deposuit et alium constituit; ex quo contingit, quod frequenter propter talem causam in uno episcopatu sunt tres vel quatuor episcopi viventes simul. Episcopos etiam depositos per eum iterum restituit suis episcopatibus, si bene solvant ei pecuniam, de qua cum ipso convenerunt. Illos vero episcopos, qui veniunt per successionem, quando non solvunt ei pecuniam, de qua cum eis convenit dictus catholicon, eos excommunicat nec dat eis chrisma, quousque solverint ei dictam pecuniam.

XCVIII. Item, catholicon Minoris Armeniae tenet apud se ulnam brachii et manum adhuc integram b. Gregorii, qui fuit catholicon et fuit ordinatus episcopus more Ecclesiae Graecae; quam ulnam et manum dictus catholicon ponit super caput et manus illorum, quos ordinat in episcopos; et dicit, quod si dictae manus impositio et brachii non fieret super caput et manus illorum, qui per eum ordinantur in episcopos, non essent ordinati in episcopos, quia impositio dicti brachii et manus faciunt consecrationes episcoporum; et propter hoc ipse nullos episcopos ut episcopos recipit, qui ordinati fuerunt per alios catholicon Armeniae Maioris, quia nullus alius catholicon, nisi ipse, dictum brachium et manum Gregorii habet.

XCIX. Item, quod episcopi armeni, venientes ad Italiam, dicunt se fuisse expulsos de episcopatibus suis per Saracenos; cum tamen hoc verum non sit; et dicunt se esse archiepiscopos, cum tamen in Armenia nullus sit archiepiscopus; ad hoc, ut possint pro pecunia vendere Religiosis mendicantibus episcopatum; et multi ex eis magnas pecunias sic exegerunt et multos episcopos taliter fecerunt; et in Curia Romana etiam ordinaverunt multos in presbyteros et diaconos, sine licentia dioecesanorum in quorum dioecesibus habitabant; et pro pecunia. Et persecuti sunt et persequuntur illos Armenos, qui secundum ritum Romanae Ecclesiae baptizantur et illos qui fidem Romanae Ecclesiae tenent; et dicunt, quod Romana Ecclesia errat, sed ipsi Armeni bonam et rectam fidem tenent.

C. Item, quod apud Armenos nulla est certa forma verborum exprimens consensum matrimonialem inter virum et uxorem; immo multi per parentes et amicos coguntur venire ad ecclesiam, ut matrimonium fiat inter eos; et quamvis unus vel ambo dicant, quod nolunt inter se matrimonialiter copulari, tamen matrimonium fit inter eos in facie ecclesiae.

CI. Item, quod inter Armenos gradus consanguinitatis et affinitatis, quod apud eos pro eodem habetur, observantur usque ad septimum gradum; si tamen aliqui, existentes in tertio gradu et infra, inter se matrimonium contrahant, permittuntur stare in tali matrimonio et non inquietantur super hoc per episcopos.

CII. Item, quod apud Armenos, si post matrimonium contractum, etiam carnali copula subsecuta et prole suscepta, viro non placeat uxor; vel e converso, ille cui non placet alter coniux, vel ambo, si sibi mutuo non placent, vadit vel vadunt ad episcopum vel sacerdotem et data pecunia et secundum quod inter se conveniunt, episcopus seu sacerdos separat dictum matrimonium et dat licentiam alteri nubendi, etiam cum altero coniuge invito; et hoc fit multotiens apud Armenos.

CIII. Item, quod apud Armenos multi sunt, qui habent multas uxores simul, quia viri habentes uxores in uno loco, cum propter mercantias vel alias transferuntur ad alia loca, accipiunt alias uxores in dictis locis in quibus se transtulerunt. In locis etiam propriis manentes multi sunt, qui duas uxores viventes simul habent, quarum unam accipiunt post aliam, etiam in facie ecclesiae talia matrimonia facientes. Spurii etiam apud eos ita succedunt in ereditate ac si legitimi essent; et promoventur sine alia dispensatione ad omnes Ordines et ad episcopatum et etiam ad statum catholicon, sicut de facto est de nepote Zachariae, qui erat filius concubinae fratris dicti Zachariae, qui promotus est in episcopum post patruum suum.

CIV. Item, quod quia Armeni dicunt, quod in ipsa unione natura humana in Christo conversa fuit in deitatem, dicti Armeni dicunt et credunt, quod Christus in Iudicio in forma divina apparebit et iudicabit et non in forma humana.

CV. Item, Armeni dicunt et tenent, quod post Generale Iudicium iusti et impii in aeternum vivent, quia ex tunc non morientur; dicunt tamen, quod ex iustis hominibus aliqui ibunt in paradisum caelestem post Iudicium et alii in paradisum terrestrem et alii in terram istam, ut supra dictum est; in quibus locis nullam poenam sustinebunt. Dicunt tamen, quod vita aeterna, etiam in illis qui ibunt ad paradisum caelestem, non consistit in Dei visione faciali et fruitione, quia Dei essentia a nulla creatura unquam videbitur, sed solummodo claritas eius.

CVI. Item, quidam catholicon Armenorum dixit et scripsit, quod in generali resurrectione omnes homines consurgent cum corporibus suis, sed tamen in coporibus eorum non erit sexuum discretio, quia si talis discretio sexuum esset inter eos, tunc viri ducerent uxores et mulieres nuberent; cuius contrarium Dominus dicit; sed resurgent viri et mulieres cum corporibus suis in alia forma, in qua non erit sexuum discretio.

CVII. Item, Armeni tenent, quod si aliquis sit in periculo moriendi et non habeat tempus recipiendi Communionem, quod faciunt crucem cum manu in terra et de quolibet brachio dictae crucis accipiunt modicum de terra et comedunt; et haec comestio terrae habetur per eos pro Communione.

CVIII. Item, quod aliqui magni homines Armeni laici dixerunt, quod sicut bestiae in morte expirant et sic moriuntur, ita et homines; et sicut bestiae, cum semel mortuae fuerunt, numquam resurgent, ita nec homines, postquam mortui fuerint, numquam resurgent.

CIX. Item quod apud Armenos nullus punitur de quocumque errore, quem teneat.

CX. Item, quod apud Armenos sunt multi alii errores a praedictis, qui errores continentur in infrascriptis libris Armenorum, quorum primus intitulatur *Tenophacer*, id est *Contra Festivitates* quas celebrant Ecclesiae Romana et Graeca. Secundus liber vocatur *Anadoarmat*, id est *Radix fidei*. Tertius liber vocatur *Joannis Mandagonensis*. Quartus liber vocatur *Joannis Ossinensis*. Quintus liber vocatur *Myascosutum*, id est *Unius locutionis*. Saxtus liber vocatur *Michaelis patriarchae Antiochen*. Septimus liber vocatur *Pauli Taronensis*. Octavus liber intitulatur *Octavensis*. Nonus liber vocatur *Matthaeus*. Decimus liber vocatur *Liber canonum Apostolorum*, in quo continentur omnes errores Armenorum. Undecimus liber dicitur *Sergniz*. Duodecimus liber dicitur *Marocha*, a nomine magistri qui sic vocabatur; in quo libro exponuntur Evangelia. Tertius-decimus liber dicitur *Nanam*, quo exponitur evangelium Joannis. Quartus-decimus dicitur *Ignadius*, in quo exponitur evangelium Lucae. Quintus-decimus vocatur *Ganazan*, idest *Liber Virgarum*. Sextus-decimus vocatur *Neguig pataracum*, in quo exponitur Missa. Decimus-septimus vocatur *Textorquire*, id est *Liber Epistolarum*. Decimus-octavus dicitur *Aismanorc*, id est *Martyrologium*. Et quod sunt plures alii libri Armenorum, in quibus multi continentur errores.

CXI. Item, Armeni dicunt, quod Christus non deposuit superflua naturae et, ut dicunt, causa est, quia corruptio talium superfluitatum est peccatorum generatio; et quia Christus peccata non fecit, ideo non est dominata sibi talis corruptio.

CXII. Item, dicunt, quod licet Christus fuerit circumcisus secundum Legem, non tamen fuit ei amputatum praeputium, quia non licebat a deificato corpore aliquid amputari; et maxime quia sic fuerat ordinatum, quod primogeniti circumciderentur findendo pellem praeputii et nihil amovendo; et Cristus fuit primogenitus.

CXIII. Item dicunt, quod Deus propter amorem hominis victus fuit, quia in suis comminationibus non fuit inventus verax, sed semipartialis; quia dixerat homini, quod moreretur si manducaret fructum vetitum et tamen non fuit totaliter mortuus post comestionem fructus, quia anima eius numquam fuit mortua. Iterum etiam nec in corpore fuit mortuus usque ad nongentesimum trigesimum annum. Item, quia animalia omnia non rebellaverunt sibi, sed necessaria in eius servitio remanserunt.

CXIV. Item dicunt, quod signum posuit Deus non occidendi Cain et ita fuit ad litteram, quia secundum eos nullus eum occidit, sed ipse de praecipitio se submisit. Ex quo innuunt Scripturam Genesis quoad haec esse falsam, quae videtur dicere quod Lamech interfecit Cain.

CXV. Item, quod cum duo episcopi graves persecutiones paterentur a catholicon Minoris Armeniae, de quorum persecutione facta est mentio supra, scripserunt supplicationem, quam miserunt regi, supplicando ei, ut faceret cessare dictum catholicon a persecutione supradicta; idem autem rex respondit eis, quod ipsi erant in posse eius et non poterant exire de partibus eius nec per mare nec per terram, nisi irent ad dictum catholicon et ei reverentiam exhiberent et reconciliarentur eidem et subditi ei in omnibus essent et de hoc darent publicam litteram, quam peteret dictus catholicon ab eis; dicens, quod ipse rex constitutus est per Armenos et non per Latinos et quamdiu viveret debebat pro fide Ecclesiae Armenorum laborare et catholicon Armenorum honorare, quia caput eius erat. Littera autem, quam petebat ab eis dictus catholicon, haec continere habebat, quod sanctam ecclesiam Armenorum deberent honorare et fidem eius praedicare et ei ut catholicon Armenorum oboedire et ipsum recognoscere solum caput eorum esse loco Dei; et quod nullum baptizarent et chrisma Armenorum honorarent, quia illud solum est verum chrisma; et quod omnia, quae ipse doceret de sancta Ecclesia Armenorum et de regulis, tanquam mandata Dei honorarent.

CXVI. Item, quod cum rex Armenorum vocatus Ethom, ut Armeni unirentur Ecclesiae Romanae, congregasset omnes episcopos Armeniae et magistros et catholicon, ut disputarent cum Legato misso eis per Romanam Ecclesiam, et facta dicta disputatione cognovisset dictus rex, quod veritatem tenebat sancta Romana Ecclesia et quod Armeni errantes erant a veritate, ex tunc reges Armeniae Minoris tenuerunt fidem sanctae Romanae Ecclesiae, sed episcopi, magistri et principes Armenorum non fuerunt de hoc contenti. Et post recessum dicti Legati, quidam magister, vocatus Vartam de Nigromonte, composuit unum librum vocatum de *Risma,* idest *Versus pedem,* contra papam et suum Legatum et contra Ecclesiam Romanam, in quo vocavit papam Romanum superbum Pharaonem, cum suis subditis in mare haeresis submersos et Legatum eius, ambaxatorem Pharaonis, fuisse reversum cum maxima verecundia; et dixit quod Ecclesia Romana erat multum decepta, quia nativitatem et aquam a maledicto Arthomono recepit; et multos alias blasphemias scripsit in dicto libro, qui magnus est. Et multi ministri Armenorum et episcopi ac presbyteri dictum librum honorant tamquam canones Apostolorum.

CXVII. Item, quod Armeni non habent omnino veram fidem, quam tenet sancta Romana Ecclesia nec Sacramenta blasphemantque sanctam Romanam Ecclesiam et papam et Cardinales, dicentes eos esse haereticos; et quod catholicon Minoris Armeniae dixit, quod papa et omnes Cardinales qualibet die plures quam ipse haberet capillos in capite faciunt homines occidere. Et licet praedicent, quod simonia non est committenda, ipsi tamen sine labe simoniae nullas gratias faciunt; et paucissimi sunt homines in Minori Armenia, praeter regem et aliquos nobiles, qui tenent fidem Romanae Ecclesia.

The Scriptorium Project is the work of a small group of lay people of various apostolic churches who are interested in the preservation, transmission, and translation of the works of the early and medieval church. Our efforts are to make the works of the church fathers accessible to anyone who might have an interest in Christian antiquities and the theological, philosophical, and moral writings that have become the bedrock of Western Civilization.

To-date, our releases have pulled from the Greek, Syriac, Georgian, Latin, Celtic, Ethiopian, and Coptic traditions of Christianity, and have been pulled from sundry local traditions and languages.

Other Selections from the Armenian Church Series:

Refutations by Eznik of Kolb (Dec. 2007)

Explanation of the Faith of the Armenian Church by Nerses IV the Gracious, Catholicos of Armenia (July 2009)

Super Quibusdam by Pope Clement VI (Nov. 2009)

The Life of Mashtots by Koriun the Iberian (Nov. 2012)

Letter to Kiwron, Catholicos of Iberia by Movses II, Catholic of Armenia (Nov. 2013)

Canons of the Synod of Partav by Sion I, Catholicos of Armenia (Dec. 2013)

The History of the Holy Cross of Aparank by St. Gregory of Narek (Feb. 2014)

Armenian Synaxarium: Volume I- Month of Navasard (Oct. 2018)

The Geography by Ananias of Shirak (Dec. 2020)

Cum Dudum: a letter to the Armenians by Pope Benedict XII (Nov. 2021)

Genealogy of the Family of St. Gregory by St. Mesrop Mashtots (Nov. 2023)

www.ingramcontent.com/pod-product-compliance
Lightning Source LLC
LaVergne TN
LVHW061040070526
838201LV00073B/5120